CREATIVE HOMEOWNER® **ULTIMATE** GUIDE TO

Drywall

PRO TIPS FOR HANGING & FINISHING

CREATIVE HOMEOWNER® ULTIMATE GUIDE TO

Drywall

PRO TIPS FOR HANGING & FINISHING

John D. Wagner

CREATIVE HOMEOWNER®, Upper Saddle River, New Jersey

Drywall: Pro Tips for Hanging and Finishing

Managing Editor: Fran J. Donegan
Associate Editor: Paul J. Rieder
Copy Editor: Douglas Cantwell
Junior Graphic Designer: Kamal Mahtani
Editorial Assistants: Evan Lambert and Daniel Lane (proofreading);
   Lauren Manoy and Robyn Poplasky (photo research)
Technical Reviewer: Hans Bakke
Illustrations: Clarke Barre (How-to and Tool Illustrations)
   Vincent Alessi, Clarke Barre, Steve Karp (Line Art)
Front Cover Photography: John Parsekian
Back Cover Photography: *top, bottom left and bottom right*
   John Parsekian; *bottom center* David Baer of Smith-Baer Studios

Creative Homeowner

VP/Publisher: Brian Toolan
VP/Editorial Director: Timothy O. Bakke
Production Manager: Kimberly H. Vivas
Art Director: David Geer
Managing Editor: Fran J. Donegan

Manufactured in the United States of America

Drywall: Pro Tips for Hanging and Finishing
Library of Congress Catalog Card Number: 2005923671
ISBN-10: 1-58011-270-6
ISBN-13: 978-1-58011-270-3

Current Printing (last digit)
10 9 8 7 6 5 4 3 2 1

CREATIVE HOMEOWNER®
A Division of Federal Marketing Corp.
24 Park Way, Upper Saddle River, NJ 07458
www.creativehomeowner.com

Acknowledgments

The author would like to thank Clayton DeKorne, David Dobbs, MaryLee McDonald, Leita Hancock, and Asa S. Wagner, as well as the editors at Creative Homeowner. The publishers would like to acknowledge the drywallers who appear in the book, Steve Veilleux and Rick Turgeon, of Friendly Drywall, East Hartford, CT, as well as the general contractor for the jobsite, Chris Caulfield. The illustrations on pages 60–62 are based on drawings provided by the United States Gypsum Co., and acknowledgment is given for their use. For providing tools for our photographs, we thank Goldblatt Tools, Hyde Tools, Makita, and Porter-Cable. For allowing us to take photographs on their premises, we thank Elmwood Supply Co., Garfield, NJ, and John Larimer.

Safety First

Although the methods in this book have been reviewed for safety, it is not possible to overstate the importance of using the safest methods you can. What follows are reminders—some do's and don'ts of work safety—to use along with your common sense.

- *Always* use caution, care, and good judgment when following the procedures described in this book.

- *Always* be sure that the electrical setup is safe, that no circuit is overloaded, and that all power tools and outlets are properly grounded. Do not use power tools in wet locations.

- *Always* read container labels on paints, solvents, and other products; provide ventilation; and observe all other warnings.

- *Always* read the manufacturer's instructions for using a tool, especially the warnings.

- Use hold-downs and push sticks whenever possible when working on a table saw. Avoid working short pieces if you can.

- *Always* remove the key from any drill chuck (portable or press) before starting the drill.

- *Always* pay deliberate attention to how a tool works so that you can avoid being injured.

- *Always* know the limitations of your tools. Do not try to force them to do what they were not designed to do.

- *Always* make sure that any adjustment is locked before proceeding. For example, always check the rip fence on a table saw or the bevel adjustment on a portable saw before starting to work.

- *Always* clamp small pieces to a bench or other work surface when using a power tool.

- *Always* wear the appropriate rubber gloves or work gloves when handling chemicals, moving or stacking lumber, working with concrete, or doing heavy construction.

- *Always* wear a disposable face mask when you create dust by sawing or sanding. Use a special filtering respirator when working with toxic substances and solvents.

- *Always* wear eye protection, especially when using power tools or striking metal on metal or concrete; a chip can fly off, for example, when chiseling concrete.

- *Never* work while wearing loose clothing, open cuffs, or jewelry; tie back long hair.

- *Always* be aware that there is seldom enough time for your body's reflexes to save you from injury from a power tool in a dangerous situation; everything happens too fast. Be alert!

- *Always* keep your hands away from the business ends of blades, cutters, and bits.

- *Always* hold a circular saw firmly, usually with both hands.

- *Always* use a drill with an auxiliary handle to control the torque when using large-size bits.

- *Always* check your local building codes when planning new construction. The codes are intended to protect public safety and should be observed to the letter.

- *Never* work with power tools when you are tired or when under the influence of alcohol or drugs.

- *Never* cut tiny pieces of wood or pipe using a power saw. When you need a small piece, saw it from a securely clamped longer piece.

- *Never* change a saw blade or a drill or router bit unless the power cord is unplugged. Do not depend on the switch being off. You might accidentally hit it.

- *Never* work in insufficient lighting.

- *Never* work with dull tools. Have them sharpened, or learn how to sharpen them yourself.

- *Never* use a power tool on a workpiece—large or small—that is not firmly supported.

- *Never* saw a workpiece that spans a large distance between horses without close support on each side of the cut; the piece can bend, closing on and jamming the blade, causing saw kickback.

- When sawing, *never* support a workpiece from underneath with your leg or other part of your body.

- *Never* carry sharp or pointed tools, such as utility knives, awls, or chisels, in your pocket. If you want to carry any of these tools, use a special-purpose tool belt that has leather pockets and holders.

Contents

Introduction **8**

CHAPTER 1

Drywall Basics 9

What is Drywall? **10**
The Benefits of Drywall **11**
How to Order and Store Drywall **11**
Gypsum Drywall Sizes and Types **12**
Selecting Drywall **14**
Cover Treatments and Specialty Drywall Panels **15**
Dealing with Moisture **18**
Edge Treatments **19**
Hanging Materials **21**
Finishing Materials **23**
Finishing Wall Panels **25**
Drywall Suspension Systems **26**

CHAPTER 2

Tools & Equipment 27

Personal Safety Tools **28**
Measuring and Marking Tools **30**
Hanging and Cutting Tools **32**
Finishing Tools **34**
Mechanical Finishing Tools **38**

CHAPTER 3

Wall & Ceiling Prep 39

Laying Out a Drywall Job **40**
Framing Tips for Drywall **43**
Checking and Correcting Alignment **45**
Furring Walls and Ceilings **50**
Steel Framing Systems **57**
Suspended Ceilings **58**

CHAPTER 4

Marking & Cutting 63

Straight Cut Lines **64**
Curved Cut Lines **69**
Special Techniques for Marking and Cutting **73**
Access Panels **76**

CHAPTER 5

Installing Drywall 77

Hanging Tips and Techniques **78**
Screws vs. Nails **81**
Hanging Drywall on a Ceiling **83**
Hanging Drywall on a Flat Wall **85**
Hanging Corners and Angles **87**
Installing Drywall on a Steel-Framed Wall **93**
Hanging a Curved Wall **94**
Hanging Drywall in Tricky Locations **97**
Building a Drywall Box around Utilities or Pipes **101**
Hanging Backer Board for Tile **103**

CHAPTER 6

Taping & Finishing 105

Taping Prep: A Checklist **106**
Taping Joints on a Flat Wall **107**
Finishing Fastener Heads **109**
Taping an Inside Corner **110**
Taping an Outside Corner **112**
Finish-Sanding **114**
Special Finishes **116**
Skim-Coating **122**

CHAPTER 7

Drywall Repairs 125

Troubleshooting **126**
Fixing and Repairing Drywall **128**
Drywall Resurfacing **140**
Dealing with Mold **143**

Fire Ratings 144
Recommended Levels for Drywall Finish 146
Resource Guide 148
Glossary 150
Credits 154
Index 155
Metric Equivalents 159

Introduction

This book is written for the do-it-yourselfer who brings beginning to intermediate building skills to drywalling projects large and small. The book is designed to walk the reader through the basics of installing gypsum drywall, step by step, from estimating, cutting, hanging, and finishing drywall panels to making basic repairs.

Of all the ways to finish the interior of your home—including plaster, wood paneling, and brick—gypsum drywall is not only the least expensive, but it's also the simplest to install. Anyone with more than a passing familiarity with simple tools, such as a power drill, handsaw, hammer, and measuring tape, should, with a little patience, be able to hang drywall just as neatly (although not nearly as quickly) as a team of professional drywall contractors.

After two introductory chapters that show you the basics of the materials and the tools involved in a normal residential drywall project, Chapter 3, "Wall & Ceiling Prep," deals with the important issues of estimating materials, making efficient layouts, and preparing the house framing for flawless drywalling. Chapter 4, "Marking & Cutting," analyzes the many methods for cutting drywall panels—including circles, archways, and other irregular lines. Chapter 5, "Installing Drywall," deals with actually hanging the panels, covering not just the basics (flat walls and ceilings) but myriad potential problem situations, such as curved walls, cathedral ceilings, and drywalling over steel framing. Chapter 6, "Taping & Finishing," covers not just the basics of spreading compound, taping, and sanding down panels, but also specialty finishes. The final chapter, "Drywall Repairs," contains numerous suggestions for making repairs—simple and complex—to damaged drywall and offers advice for problems that you may encounter during your installation.

Each step-by-step project in the book begins with a suggested list of the tools and materials necessary to complete the work. Each task also begins by rating the level of difficulty of the work to be done. The level of difficulty is indicated by one, two, or three hammers:

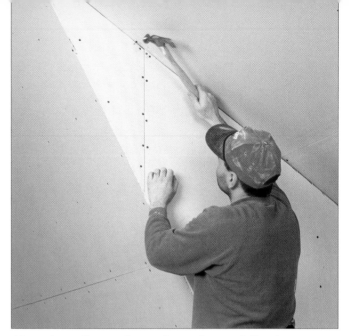

Most drywalling tasks involve ordinary skills—hammering nails, cutting panels, and sanding, for example.

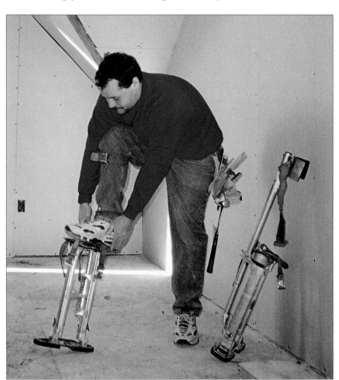

Although stilts are not required, drywalling can be much easier with the use of such special equipment.

Easy, even for most beginners.

Challenging, but can be handled by do-it-yourselfers with basic tools and carpentry skills.

Difficult, but still doable by experienced do-it-yourselfers who have mastered basic construction skills and have the tools and time for the job. Consider consulting a specialist.

Chapter 1

Drywall Basics

Drywall, also known as plasterboard, wallboard, or gypsum board, is by far the most popular and practical material for surfacing interior walls. Nowadays it's rare to find a finished wall, either in a home or a business, that hasn't been surfaced with some kind of drywall product. Drywall is durable, easy to finish with paint or wallpaper, simple to repair, and you don't need to be an expert to install it. Perfectly flat, plumb walls are within the reach of any handy, patient homeowner willing to invest the time.

*B*efore drywall was developed in the 1930s, plaster was the most widely used wallcovering and the only economical alternative to expensive solid wood paneling.

Plaster can be extremely durable—some plaster walls have survived for hundreds of years—but it tends to be brittle unless it's applied over a truly rigid frame. Older homes (generally pre-World War II) were structured for plaster. They were built using a system called *balloon framing*, which called for long lengths of full-size 2×4 studs that ran from the foundation to the roof rafters.

Since then, contractors have preferred framing one floor at a time using shorter studs. This more economical platform system yielded a strong frame but less rigid walls, which created the need for a sturdier wall-covering—one of the many reasons for the development of drywall.

Labor time became a factor as well. In the old days, builders nailed wooden lath to the studs and joists, and then applied plaster to the lath in a three-coat process. The first coat, called the scratch coat, was forced into the gaps, locking itself to the lath. The brown coat covered the scratch coat, and the thin white coat went on last for finish. The process ate

Rock-solid walls *begin, appropriately, with rock—namely, the mineral gypsum. Powdered, mixed with water, and poured between sheets of paper, gypsum forms the solid core of a drywall panel.*

up a considerable number of man-hours. On top of that, lath did not always present a flat surface.

Eventually the twin economic pressures of labor and material began to put the squeeze on plaster. Builders were demanding a wallcovering that went up easily, required no lathing, and presented a flat surface without painstaking finish work.

In the early 1930s, United States Gypsum Company (USG) invented Rocklath, a paper-and-gypsum board that attached to the studs as an underlayment. The plaster bonded directly to it, making plastering a little faster and easier, but the job still took a lot of time even without nailing up lath.

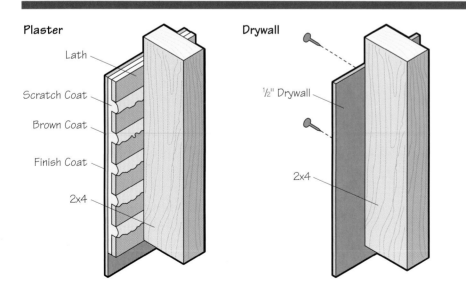

Plaster vs. Drywall. *Plaster walls (left) consist of a lath base and a scratch coat, a brown coat, and a finish coat of plaster. Drywall (right) has largely replaced plaster because of its ease of installation and low cost.*

What is Drywall?

Near the end of the 1930s, USG developed the Sheetrock Drywall System—thicker gypsum panels that could be taped together neatly and required no plaster top coat. Although it wasn't used widely until the postwar housing boom, Sheetrock evolved into the more refined paper-coated gypsum board that covers the walls and ceilings of most homes today.

Gypsum drywall is converted rock: it starts out as calcium sulfate dihydrate, or hydrous calcium sulfate ($CaSO_4 \cdot 2H_2O$), also known as gypsum, a mineral that ranges from almost black to white in color. As the chemical formula indicates, gypsum naturally contains water. In fact, water makes up about 21 percent of gypsum's weight and about 50 percent of its volume as water of crystallization. This is what gives drywall its fire resistance. The crystallized water in gypsum will turn to steam when exposed to extreme heat, keeping fire from spreading and the temperature down for a limited period of time.

The gypsum, once mined, is crushed, dried, and ground to a powder. This powder is then heated to drive off most of the remaining carbon dioxide and water, at which point it has been dehydrated to form calcium sulfate hemihydrate ($CaSO_4$-$\frac{1}{2}H_2O$), better known as Plaster of Paris. This calcined gypsum is then mixed with water, which rehydrates it back into calcium sulfate dihydrate. The resulting slurry is poured between two sheets of heavy paper with folded edges, sandwiched flat, and allowed to set. The boards are then cut, dried, and (if they don't require a special finish) packaged for sale.

Gypsum deposits occur in two large regions in the United States, as well as in Nova Scotia and Mexico.

The Benefits of Drywall

Why use gypsum wallboard instead of plaster? Besides the time saved during its installation, drywall offers a number of other benefits: it's fire-resistant; it helps deaden sound; it's durable; and it's easy to repair. Specialty drywall (with foil faces and a fiberglass core) can have a fire-resistance rating of 4 hours or even higher, depending on its thickness. Drywall makes a home quieter because gypsum naturally resists sound transmission. It resists fracturing, withstands a good deal of typical household abuse, and can be repaired easily using drywall patches to mend holes or a simple application of joint compound to smooth out dings and dents.

In addition to these benefits, drywall's paper facing readily takes a number of finishes, including paint, texturing, and wallpaper. Certain drywall products (some of which contain no gypsum) can serve as an underlayment for tile. These water-resistant drywall and cementitious (cement-based) panels go by trade names such as Blueboard and Durock Cement Board.

How to Order & Store Drywall

Have your drywall delivered only when you are ready to use it, after the framers are done and the wiring and plumbing have been roughed in. Panels get damaged if you store them on a job site for too long, especially if workers are walking through, carrying unwieldy tools and snaking extension cords. Repairing even minor damage will require multiple coats of joint compound.

Drywall is heavy. A 4 × 8-foot panel of $\frac{1}{2}$-inch gypsum drywall weighs about 54 pounds. Panels are shipped as two-sheet units that are joined by a strip of paper at each end. You tear off or slice the paper with a utility knife. One strong person can pick up a single sheet, but you'll want to recruit an assistant if you have to handle more than a few sheets. Don't attempt to move two-sheet units without help.

If you order ten sheets or more, drywall is typically delivered on a boom truck with an articulated crane arm that can lift it to a second story. The crane arm cradles the drywall just outside the window for easy removal. (Check to make sure the window area is clear of utility wires.) Window delivery decreases labor and eliminates the hazard of carrying panels up the stairs, which can damage or bow them, to say nothing of potential back injuries to the workers.

***Using a boom truck** is the easiest way to get drywall into an upper floor. Here, a lumberyard's boom truck lifts panels to where they can be pulled through a second-story window.*

If possible, it's best to take delivery through a window before the jambs have been installed. If the windows are already in place and are large enough, remove the sashes to avoid potential damage. This will take some time, but it still beats carrying panels from the first floor up a narrow staircase or shredding the edges of your stock, which creates even more work.

For first-floor delivery, carry the panels through a doorway, or position the boom truck's crane near an open window and pass the panels through. If you have to carry stock through a finished or carpeted area, lay down plastic or plywood to protect the floor.

STORAGE
When storing drywall, distribute the panels throughout the house to spread the weight around—50 panels can weigh over a ton. Estimate the number and types of panels each room requires; that way, you can distribute them upon delivery and avoid double-handling. In most rooms, the ceiling goes up first, so you'll want to off-load these panels last. This will place them at the top or front of the stack.

If space is tight, stack panels on edge lengthwise against the wall that you will drywall last, with the good, or *face,* side out. Choose a location in which the panels can sit perpendicular to the floor joists to help distribute weight evenly. If you intend to lay your stock flat on the floor, sweep the area thoroughly beforehand to remove any debris that might press into the panels and cause a blemish, scratch, or dent. Always store panels back side down on the floor.

Lumber should be blocked up off the floor—but not drywall. The panels will sag between blocks, and the resulting bows will make installation difficult later on. Once drywall is on site, keep the temperature between 55 and 70 degrees Fahrenheit. As with any construction material, inspect the panels upon delivery to make sure they are in pristine condition. Refuse to accept damaged panels, and remember to ask for credit for any stock you have to return.

Gypsum Drywall Sizes & Types

LENGTH
Gypsum drywall comes in 8-, 9-, 10-, 12-, 14-, and 16-foot lengths. It's best to use longer panels where possible to minimize the number of seams. Fewer seams mean less taping and less chance that irregular seams will show through the finished wall.

THICKNESS

Gypsum drywall comes in ¼-, ⅜-, ½-, and ⅝-inch thicknesses. Here's a look at common applications for each thickness.

◤ **¼-Inch-Thick Drywall:** Available in 8- and 10-foot panels, this stock is used for curved walls and sometimes for resurfacing over plaster or other solid-surface walls. Handle these panels carefully; because of their thinness, they can easily whip like sheet metal while being carried and can break apart. On curved walls, even a short length of ¼-inch-thick drywall requires a maximum stud spacing of 16 inches on center; it will noticeably bow on 24-inch on-center studs. When installing over a solid surface, use adhesive to help hold the panels in place. At 1.2 pounds per square foot, a 4 × 8-foot sheet of ¼-inch-thick drywall weighs about 38 pounds.

◤ **⅜-Inch-Thick Drywall:** Available in 8-, 9-, 10-, 12-, and 14-foot lengths, this material is ideal for remodeling partition walls and for patching areas where old plaster has been removed. A ⅜-inch thickness requires a maximum stud spacing of 16 inches on-center. At 1.4 pounds per square foot, a 4 × 8-foot panel weighs about 45 pounds.

◤ **½-Inch-Thick Drywall:** Available in 8-, 9-, 10-, 12-, 14-, and 16-foot lengths, this most common thickness works well for both walls and ceilings. Stud spacing can be 24 inches on center, unless the panels are hung with their long edges parallel to the ceiling joists. In this case, stick with 16-inch on-center framing to prevent sagging. At 1.7 pounds per square foot, a 4 × 8-foot sheet weighs about 54 pounds.

◤ **⅝-Inch-Thick Drywall:** Available in 8-, 9-, 10-, 12-, and 14-foot lengths, this stock, sometimes called firewall drywall, can be used in walls and ceilings. Like ½-inch, it can be hung on 24-inch on-center

The length of gypsum drywall goes far beyond the 8 ft. that most suppliers have in stock. Panels as long as 14 and 16 ft. are available to finish long walls with a minimal number of seams.

framing unless it is hung horizontally. The extra thickness improves sound dampening and resistance to sagging. In many areas, ⅝-inch drywall is required by code because of its superior fire resistance. At 2.3 pounds per square foot, a 4 × 8-foot panel weighs about 73 pounds.

◤ **Double-Layer Systems:** To increase a wall's fire resistance and sound-dampening qualities, you can apply a double layer of drywall. A double-layer application also offers superior resistance to sagging and cracking (especially when adhesives are used). The bottom, or base, layer is covered by a top, or face, layer. Typically, adhesive is used between layers to add even more wall strength.

WIDTH

Common gypsum drywall panels measure 48 inches wide. Two stacked horizontal pieces or one vertical 96-inch length will span 8 feet, the height of a common ceiling. With some ceiling heights now measuring 8½ or 9 feet high, manufacturers have started producing 54-inch-wide panels. Two of these will cover a 9-foot wall.

Selecting Drywall

As discussed on page 13, drywall panels are available in a variety of sizes. The standard for most residential work is the $\frac{1}{2}$-inch-thick panel. Larger $\frac{5}{8}$-inch panels are not usually used in houses due to the extra weight and cost. It may not seem like much, but that extra $\frac{1}{8}$ of an inch makes the larger panels much heavier and harder to handle, especially for someone working alone. The lighter $\frac{3}{8}$-inch-thick panels are good for resurfacing work when a wall is so scarred that spackling cannot save it. The $\frac{1}{4}$-inch-thick panel is the most economical, but most people, including most pros, don't like to use them because the sheets are very whippy and snap too easily during handling. Of course, be sure to check local building codes when planning a large-scale new construction or remodeling project.

As is the case with plywood and other construction sheet goods, the standard size for drywall panels is 4 × 8 feet, although other sizes are available. (See "Gypsum Drywall Sizes and Types," page 12.) The standard size works well with both 16-inch and 24-inch-on-center framing.

Two common variations of standard panels are manufactured with qualities that improve drywall performance in key areas: panels impregnated with fire retardants, referred to as FC or fire code panels—see "Fire Resistant Drywall," page 16—and drywall panels that are treated to resist moisture—see "Dealing with Moisture," page 18.

From the standpoint of handling, smaller sheets are best—easier to carry and install. But from the standpoint of taping and finishing joints, larger sheets are better because they cover more wall area. The best approach is to use the largest sheets practicable—large enough to eliminate some seams and taping time but not large enough to create major handling problems.

Drywall Types: A—$\frac{1}{4}$ in., **B**—$\frac{3}{8}$ in., **C**—$\frac{1}{2}$ in., **D**—$\frac{5}{8}$ in. fire code, **E**—$\frac{1}{2}$ in. water-resistant

Specially-made flexible panels cover curved walls and archways without requiring kerfing or soaking with water.

Cover Treatments & Specialty Drywall Panels

◤ **Flexible Drywall:** This ¼-inch-thick material is intended for tighter curved-wall or archway applications and is often applied in two layers. Flexible gypsum drywall has a stronger liner and face paper than regular ¼-inch-thick drywall and resists cracking more effectively.

◤ **Abuse-Resistant Drywall:** Compared with standard gypsum panels, abuse-resistant panels have a heavier paper covering and a reinforced core. These panels give greater resistance to damage. Available in ½- and ⅝-inch thicknesses, this stock is recommended for playrooms, high-traffic hallways, and garage and basement walls that are likely to sustain damage from bikes or tools.

For this type of usage, manufacturers have recently developed a gypsum/wood fiber backing that resists dents and punctures better than paper and increases panel strength. Stock with this backing costs more than ordinary gypsum drywall and usually must be special-ordered.

◤ **Moisture-Resistant Drywall:** Also called MR (moisture-resistant) board, WR (water-resistant) board, Greenboard, or Blueboard, this gypsum drywall (which has a pale green or blue face) resists moisture but is not waterproof. It can withstand the high levels of humidity that often occur in bathrooms, kitchens, and laundry rooms. These panels make a good base for any kind of tile attached with a mastic. Avoid hanging the material over an existing vapor barrier, because this would trap moisture, causing the drywall to degrade over time. Moisture-

The Pros Know

Don't tear apart your bathroom with a crowbar and then drive down to the local home center assuming they'll have those ⅝-inch Type X panels and 10-foot MR boards that you'll need in stock. Many suppliers carry a limited variety of panels on the floor, and you'll either have to wait for the ones you want to be ordered (and live with your mess) or take what they have.

Flexible Drywall. *Flexible ¼-in. drywall is a convenient product for curved walls and double-layered installations, but ordinary walls call for a thicker panel.*

Abuse-Resistant Drywall. *For rooms with lots of traffic or the potential for wall damage, abuse-resistant drywall can withstand moderate impacts without being damaged.*

Moisture-Resistant Drywall. *While not waterproof, this material is a good choice for use in high-humidity areas such as kitchens and bathrooms; it's used to support ceramic tile behind a kitchen sink, for example.*

resistant drywall can be finished and painted or wallpapered like regular drywall panels. It should be installed on studs framed 16 inches on center.

◣ **Cement Board:** Also called cementitious panel, Durock, Hardibacker, WonderBoard, or Dens-Shield, this ½- or ⅝-inch-thick stock comes in 5- or 8-foot lengths and in widths of 32, 36, and 48 inches. Unlike gypsum-based products, this material consists of a portland cement core sandwiched between layers of a polymer-coated glass fiber mesh. It provides excellent fire and water resistance and makes an ideal backing for tile, especially in high-moisture areas such as bathroom and kitchen walls and floors. It also offers a superior underlayment for use with slate and quarry tile. Each cement-based board has a rough and a smooth side. Install the rough side facing outward when attaching tiles with mortar (such as QuickSet) or with the smooth side out when using adhesive or mastic. Some cementitious products are UL-listed for use as wall shield and floor protectors in rooms with exposed heaters and wood stoves. Maximum stud spacing for application is 16 inches on center.

◣ **Fire-Resistant Drywall:** Available in ½- and ⅝-inch thicknesses, this material, known as Firecode Core, Fire-Shield, Fireguard, or Fi-Rock, is fire resistant. This means that it meets or exceeds the ASTM C36 rating for Type X fire-resistant gypsum board, which specifies that glass fibers be embedded in its core, enabling it to resist fire for a certain amount of time beyond conventional gypsum drywall. Typically, a ½-inch-thick panel is rated to contain a fire for 45 minutes, a ⅝-inch-thick panel for 60 minutes. Codes often require these panels for party walls (between condos or apartments), for ceilings that adjoin other units, and for rooms that are susceptible to fire, such as furnace rooms, attached garages, and kitchens.

Cement Board. *These panels are for areas that need extra resistance to fire or water damage. They are also an excellent tile backer for high-moisture areas such as bathroom and kitchen walls and as an underlayment for slate and quarry tile.*

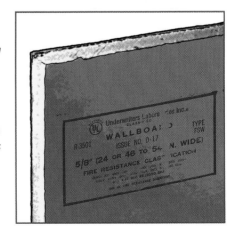

Fire-Resistant Drywall. *These panels can contain a fire for a certain amount of time. Building codes often require fire-resistant panels in party walls between apartments or in common walls between a house and an attached garage.*

1 Drywall Basics

■ **Foil-Backed Board:** Where a vapor barrier is required, foil-backed panels may be useful. This stock is made by laminating aluminum foil (backed by kraft paper) to the surface of a gypsum drywall panel. The foil face increases the insulation value of the drywall and helps create a vapor barrier if the foil face is placed against the studs on the interior side of exterior walls. As with any vapor barrier, this helps prevent moisture in the living area from entering the stud bays. Avoid using foil-backed panels as a base for tiles or in any area where another wall covering could trap moisture within the core of the panel. Also, avoid using this material in air-conditioned structures that ordinarily withstand frequent high outdoor temperatures and humidity.

■ **Sound-Deadening Board:** Sound-deadening in drywall application has more to do with wall design than with the use of any particular drywall product. Sound-deadening materials are available, but they usually are sold as insulation, such as USG's Thermafiber. Sound-deadening techniques typically combine the use of two layers of drywall with a sound-deadening blanket, an acoustical sealant, and a wall system of studs and metal channels that creates baffles within a wall.

■ **Ceiling Panels:** A number of manufacturers make special panels for use in ceiling applications, particularly when the ceiling is built with wider truss spans (24 inches on center). Designed to be both lighter and stronger than standard stock; these panels resist sagging, install more easily, and in some cases cost less than regular gypsum drywall.

■ **Vinyl-Faced Panels:** Available in a wide variety of colors and patterns, these gypsum drywall panels are

Foil-Backed Board. Many fire-resistant products have a kraft-backed aluminum foil layer. Besides preventing the spread of fire, the foil forms an excellent vapor barrier.

Vinyl-Faced Panels. These pre-decorated panels, usually seen in commercial settings, have a vinyl face that does not need to be painted. These panels are trimmed with plastic moldings rather than tape and joint compound.

attached using adhesive and special fasteners (similar to finishing nails) and require no edge or joint treatments because they're trimmed with specially designed vinyl moldings. Butted end joints are difficult to conceal, so avoid using these panels in rooms or on ceilings where end joints will be visible. Panels typically come in $\frac{1}{2}$-inch thicknesses and in 4-, 8-, 9-, and 10-foot lengths.

■ **Gypsum Lath:** Gypsum lath serves as a base for veneer plaster. Sold under such names as Rocklath, Kal-Kore, and Cameo, gypsum lath provides a fire-resistant underlayment for trowel applications of plaster, replacing wooden lath. It comes in $\frac{1}{2}$- and $\frac{3}{8}$-inch thicknesses, with panel sizes ranging from 16 × 48 inches to 25 × 96 inches. Although not identical to drywall, gypsum lath can have a gypsum core and often is faced with absorbent paper. The paper draws water away from the freshly applied plaster to keep it from slumping, while several additional layers of treated paper prevent this moisture from seeping into the panel's core.

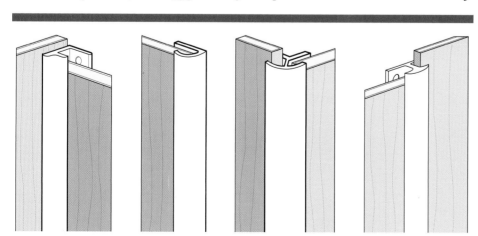

***Special moldings** finish the edges and joints where predecorated panels meet on the wall and at corners, and where the panels end. These panels are usually installed vertically.*

Dealing with Moisture

Moisture damages drywall surfaces. Anyone who has ever experienced a leaky roof or pipe knows that the repair to the source of the leak is often followed up with a repair to the damaged wall or ceiling. Even minor leaks can, over time, cause paint to peel and the outer layer of paper on a standard drywall panel to delaminate. Excessive moisture can cause the panel to crumble.

For years drywall manufacturers have offered products designed for installation in high-moisture areas such as bathrooms and kitchens. (See "Cover Treatments and Specialty Drywall Panels," pages 15-16.) But tighter construction practices of recent years have led to additional moisture problems. In some homes, the increased levels of humidity generated by normal everyday activities such as cooking, drying clothes, and showering can lead to wet wall and ceiling surfaces and to the formation of mold. An undetected leak can also lead to the formation of mold. Mold spores will grow on any wet surface, including the back of wallpaper and drywall surfaces inside wall cavities.

Although it is unsightly, most molds are not dangerous to most people. However, many people are sensitive to mold spores. Reactions can range from hay fever-type symptoms to more extreme reactions such as asthma attacks in people with asthma who are allergic to mold.

Ventilation Basics

You can avoid many moisture problems in new and remodeled homes through proper ventilation. Kitchens and bathrooms should contain ventilation systems that vent moisture and stale air directly outdoors. Ventilation fans are rated by the amount of air they move in cubic feet per minute (CFM).

Kitchens
Ranges and cooktops installed against a wall
Light cooking: 40 CFM
Medium to heavy cooking: 100 to 150 CFM

Ranges and cooktops installed in islands and peninsulas:
Light cooking: 50 CFM
Medium to heavy cooking: 150 to 300 CFM

Bathrooms
CFM = Room Width (feet) x Room Length (feet) x 1.1

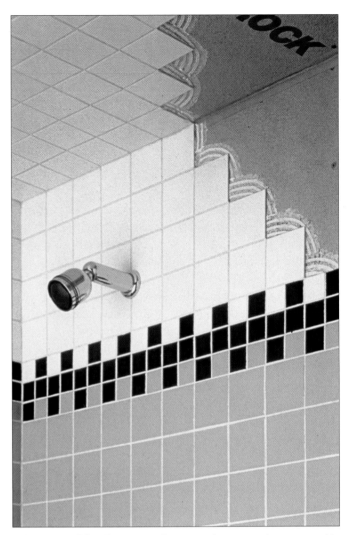

Waterproof Applications. *A proper tile system that starts with waterproof cement-based backerboard is the secret to avoiding moisture problems in shower surrounds.*

To help prevent the formation of mold, be sure your home is properly ventilated. Clothes dryers, kitchen ranges, and bathrooms should be vented to the outdoors. There are also products designed for increased water resistance.

Paperless Panels. Some manufacturers offer drywall panels that do not contain the typical paper facing. Removing the organic paper means there is nothing for mold spores to feed upon, nor is there the possibility of the paper pulling away from the gypsum core. Moisture will not affect these panels as it does typical drywall panels. Some manufacturers replace the paper with a glass-fiber matt; others use a gypsum formulation that provides a smooth surface. The new generation of paperless panels comes in standard sizes. Installation and finishing options are the same for new paperless panels as they are for traditional drywall panels.

Edge Treatments

Drywall can have any of four edge treatments: tapered, square, tongue-and-groove, or beveled.

The most common of these, which comes standard on regular gypsum panels, is a **tapered** edge. On the face side of the panel (the side that faces the room), the long edges taper slightly to form a recess about $1/20$ inch deep. This allows tape and joint compound to be applied flush with the face of the panel. The shorter ends of regular panels, however, are square.

Square-edged drywall has edges identical in thickness to the body of the panel. With this material, all joints are similar to those created when you join regular panels end to end. With practice, you can finish adjoining square edges neatly with tape and joint compound. However, square-edged panels are best used where no finishing is required, as in the bottom layer of a two-layer application.

Tongue-and-groove drywall panels have interlocking V-shape edges. Finishing these edges takes serious skill, and tongue-and-groove stock is rarely used in applications that require finishing. The locking tongue and groove provides resistance against wind and water, which explains why tongue-and-groove

Corner bead and other acessories provide the necessary finishing touches for a drywall job.

panels are recommended for use under some exterior siding, masonry veneer, stucco, and shingles.

Beveled edges, which you don't see that often, are meant to be left unfinished to give the room a paneled look. Unfortunately, in rooms that won't take all full panels, it's difficult to lay out the panels so that each joint will have two clean beveled edges.

METAL AND PLASTIC ACCESSORIES

Drywall edges and butt ends don't always meet in perfectly straight, tightly made seams that can be finished with tape and joint compound. Sometimes you need to fasten metal or plastic accessories to the panels (or to the framing beneath the panels)—for example, to help reinforce an outside corner or protect a joint where drywall abuts another surface.

Corner bead is an L-shaped piece of galvanized steel with holes drilled in its flanges. This material reinforces the outside corner where two drywall panels meet. After you attach corner bead by clinching or by nailing or screwing through the drywall into the framing, you finish it using joint compound but no tape. When properly installed and finished, these steel angles strengthen the corner and define it with a clean straight line. The *nose*, or raised bead, also acts as a kind of screed guide for your knife when applying joint compound.

Square Edge

Tapered Edge

Tongue & Groove

Edge Treatments. *The three most common edges: square edges (which create butt joints), tapered edges (ideal for drywall panels that will be finished with tape and joint compound), and tongue-and-groove (common with vapor-barrier-creating drywall panels).*

J-bead (also called J-trim) wraps around the edge of a gypsum drywall panel to protect it from damage or disintegration. It's used in places where a drywall panel abuts a brick wall, window jamb, shower stall, or other structure. To attach J-bead, you drive screws or nails through the face of the panel and the bead's back flange.

There are two types of J-bead. *Finishing-type* has a front flange that requires finishing with joint compound. The raised bead on this flange acts as a guide for your joint-compound knife. *Reveal-type* J-bead, on the other hand, is not designed to be finished with joint compound. Because J-bead wraps snugly around the panel edge, it must be matched to the thickness of the gypsum drywall panel. Use a ¼-inch J-bead for ¼-inch drywall, a ⅜-inch J-bead for ⅜-inch panel, and so on.

L-bead, less common than J-bead, also allows a panel to abut a window or door casing. However, it is used with casings that aren't designed to cover the drywall's edge. L-bead creates a recess between the casing and the panel.

Metal Corner Bead No. 800 Corner Bead Metal J-Bead (Finishing Type) Metal J-Bead (Reveal Type) Plastic J-Bead (Reveal Type)

Attach metal corner bead to outside corners with drywall nails about every 6 inches. The raised bead guides the drywall knife to create smooth finished edges for joint compound.

J-bead is used where drywall panels abut non-drywalled surfaces. One type of J-bead (finishing type) is finished with joint compound. The other type (reveal type) is left as is, with its finished flange facing out.

Bullnose corner bead and **flexible bead** are made of vinyl. Bullnose bead provides a rounded 90-degree corner for a "soft" appearance. Flexible bead is used in any joint that involves a curved outside corner, as in an archway or above a curved window. This L-shaped bead has one notched and one solid flange. As you apply the bead to the corner, the notches spread out to adjust for the curve, and you then screw through the flanges to hold the bead in place.

A product called **arch bead** is also available for finishing curved edges. Both the vinyl bead and the metal, V-shaped sides are flexible and can be

     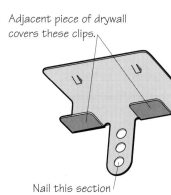

Adjacent piece of drywall covers these clips.

Nail this section into stud or plate.

Metal L-Bead   Plastic L-Bead

L-bead *is an edge finish that is installed where drywall abuts a non-drywalled finished edge. The flange on the face of the drywall is finished with joint compound.*

Bullnose corner bead *is a vinyl edge-finish treatment that provides a soft 90° corner. It is finished in the same way as metal corner bead.*

Flexible vinyl corner bead *is used to finish the joints at the top of arched doors and windows or where curved edges need finishing.*

Arch bead *provides a curved edge that can be finished with joint compound. Its most common application would be at the top of an arch.*

Drywall clips *provide backing for drywall edges that miss framing members. They are attached to an adjacent stud or plate.*

Wire shields should be installed on the face of a stud if there is a risk of a screw or nail penetrating pipes or wiring running within the stud wall.

120°

Flexible Metal Corner Tape

Flexible metal corner tape is used where the angle of an outside or inside corner exceeds 90 degrees. The corner tape has metal strips running down its center.

pressed into any curved or irregular shape without having to be cut. Arch bead is available at many home centers.

Drywall clips are L-shaped pieces of metal or plastic, with each wing of the clip measuring about 2 inches wide. They are used most commonly to attach partition walls to floor and ceiling framing. You install these clips to provide a screwing base and backing on a drywall edge that doesn't face onto a stud or joist.

Flexible metal corner tape typically measures 2 inches wide and has two $1/2$-inch-wide galvanized metal strips running along each side of a center crease. It is designed for use on outside and inside corners that form an angle greater than 90 degrees, replacing corner bead. Install it with the metal side facing inward, and apply joint compound as you would to conventional paper tape.

Wire shields, also called *nail plates*, are small $1^1/2$-inch (stud-width) by 2-inch metal plates with four pointed legs that get hammered into the stud faces. Install shields wherever a fastener might protrude into wiring or piping running within a stud.

Hanging Materials

Drywall is attached to studs and joists with nails or screws. Screws have become the preferred fastener because they are easy to install, provide more holding power than nails, and don't disturb the framing or furring when applied. The pounding of drywall nails can shake furring loose, cause nails already in place to pop, and even move studs out of alignment. In addition, screws can be removed (in case you have to remove and recut a panel), and screwhead depth is easier to control, especially with screw-gun clutches that can be set to release once a screw has reached a desired depth. (Nailhead depth must be gauged correctly by eye every time.)

NAILS

There are three types of nails used to fasten drywall to studs and ceiling joists: ringed nails, cement-coated nails, and cooler nails, each of which has a minimum $1/4$-inch-diameter head. Nail length varies according to the thickness of your drywall. For $3/8$-inch-thick panels, use $1^1/8$-inch nails; for $1/2$-inch, use $1^1/4$-inch nails; for $5/8$-inch, use $1^3/8$-inch nails. Drive the nails with a bell- or convex-faced drywall hammer. The wide, rounded crosshatched, heads on these hammers create a dimple around the nailhead that facilitates the application of joint compound. All nails are designed to attach drywall to wooden, not steel, studs. If you're attaching drywall to metal studs or furring strips, you must use screws.

A **ringed nail** has threads that resist withdrawal. **Cement-coated nails** have smooth shanks but are coated with cement to increase resistance. **Cooler nails** resemble ringed nails but lack the raised rings.

Ringed Nail

Cement-coated Nail

Cooler Nail

Nails. Three types of drywall nails: Ringed nails (left) are threaded to resist pullout. Cement-coated nails (center) use cement coating to add friction to the nail's bite, defeating pullout. Cooler nails (right) are smooth-shank nails used in drywall applications where risk of pullout is not great.

They have a head and shaft designed especially for fastening drywall.

Be careful to stop driving the nailhead once you've dimpled the drywall's face. An overdriven nail will tear the face paper, which will make finishing difficult and reduce the nail's holding power. The same holds true for nails that are driven in at an angle.

SCREWS

Three types of Phillips-head screws are used to fasten drywall to studs and joists: Type W (wood), Type G (gypsum), and Type S (steel) screws. When fastening drywall to wood studs or joists, use **Type W screws.** Use **Type G screws** to fasten one drywall panel to another in a double-layer application. To fasten panels to metal studs or furring, use **Type S screws**—preferably self-tapping screws, which have winged tips that drill through steel quickly.

As with nails, drive the screws far enough to create a dimple, but don't tear the paper. (You can outfit a power drill with a clutch that will release the screw when it is driven to a certain depth.)

Screws. Three types of drywall screws: Type W screws are designed for attaching drywall to wood studs. Type G screws are for attaching drywall to drywall. Type S screws—normal and self-tapping—are designed for attaching drywall to steel studs.

Fastener Type	Drywall Thickness	Minimum Fastener Length
Type W screws *(coarse thread)*	3/8 in.	1 in.
	1/2 in.	1 1/8 in.
	3/8 in.	1 1/4 in.
Type S screws *(self-tapping)*	3/8 in.	1 in.
	1/2 in.	1 1/4 in.
	5/8 in.	1 3/8 in.
Ring-shank nails *(wooden studs only)*	3/8 in.	1 1/8 in.
	1/2 in.	1 1/4 in.
	5/8 in.	1 3/8 in.

Adhesives. Drywall adhesive can help reduce the number of fasteners required to attach drywall. Drywall adhesive is properly applied in a bead form, and when the drywall panel is pressed into place, the adhesive should flatten out across the face of the stud, with no excess oozing out.

ADHESIVES

Many drywall applications call for an adhesive in addition to screws or nails. Adhesives can be used to fasten drywall to another gypsum board, as well as to wood, masonry, or metal. Although they generally are not essential, adhesives can double a wall's tensile strength, increase its sheer strength by 50 percent, and dampen sound transmission. If you're applying panels over existing walls, such as wood paneling or old plaster, adhesives can reduce the number of fasteners required by as much as 75 percent, which also minimizes the finishing work.

Application. Before you start, trim the adhesive tube to a diameter that will produce the proper size of bead. (When you attach a panel to a stud, the adhesive should squeeze out to cover the entire face of the stud but not ooze beyond it.) Cut the adhesive tube's nozzle in a V shape to get a truly round bead. Apply the adhesive right to the face of the studs with a caulking gun. Run the adhesive bead to within 6 inches of the ends of each frame member. Fasten the drywall to the adhesive immediately, before it has a chance to set up (within about 15 minutes). Figure on using about four gallons of adhesive for every 1,000 square feet of drywall coverage.

Types. You can select from three types of adhesive. Use a *stud adhesive* (construction adhesive) in combination with nails or screws to attach drywall to wood or metal studs or directly to concrete or masonry. You dispense it with a caulking gun. An ideal bead measures 1/4 to 3/8 inch wide. Use a *laminating adhesive* between layers of drywall in double-layer applications, and also to attach drywall to concrete or rigid foam insulation (polystyrene or urethane). Apply a bead of adhesive at the location of each frame member when attaching the face layer in a multilayer application. Use a *contact cement* to attach vinyl-faced panels to a drywall base. It can be rolled on, but you should always follow the manufacturer's instructions.

Finishing Materials

To finish seams and cover screw- or nailheads, you'll need to seal the panels' adjoining edges with drywall tape and apply various layers of joint compound. This part of the job will stand out most noticeably if you make a mistake. It takes a good eye and some skill to make joints that appear perfectly flat.

Finishing Materials. To complete your drywalling job, you'll need to apply drywall tape and joint compound. You can also finish the whole room with a texturing compound.

TAPE TYPES

Drywall tape, either paper or fiberglass, is used as a base for multiple layers of joint compound. For years, paper tape was the only product you could buy. Today, many professional drywallers (those who have lots of practice) use the more expensive self-sticking fiberglass tape (also called mesh) for many applications.

Paper tape measures 2 inches wide and comes in rolls up to 500 feet long. It has a crease down the center, which makes for easier folding on corner applications. If you're a beginning drywaller, you'll have an easier time with paper tape. It resists wrinkling better than fiberglass tape, and it trims more easily to the right length—just use the edge of your taping knife to cut it. Paper tape takes a bit longer to apply than fiberglass tape, however, because you have to spread a base layer of joint compound before applying the tape to the seam.

Some manufacturers perforate paper tape with weep holes to allow joint compound to saturate it. Perforated tape costs a little more than the standard type, but it makes the job of bedding and covering the seams slightly easier.

Fiberglass tape is a net-like mesh that comes in $1\frac{1}{2}$- to 2-inch-wide rolls up to 300 feet long. You simply apply this self-sticking material to a dry seam, and then follow it with multiple coats of joint compound. Non-self-sticking fiberglass tape can be stapled in place over a dry seam.

Tape Types. Fiberglass mesh drywall tape (left) is treated with a mild adhesive. The tape sticks in place along drywall seams and is then covered with three layers of joint compound. Flexible metal corner tape (center) is used on outside and inside corners greater or less than 90 degrees. Paper drywall tape (right) is embedded in a base coat of joint compound and then covered with two more coats of joint compound.

JOINT COMPOUNDS AND TEXTURES

Joint compound, sometimes called mud, comes in two general formulas, each of which includes several types that have specific applications. The two general formulas are vinyl-based drying-type compound, which hardens as the water medium dries, and setting-type compound, which is hardened by a chemical reaction that is catalyzed by water.

Drying-type compound is sold in both powdered and premixed form. The latter, which comes in 1-, 2½-, and 5-gallon buckets, is more commonly used today. Of the three basic types of this formula, *taping compound* is applied first to adhere the tape to the drywall seam. *Topping compound* is used for both the middle coat (often called the filler coat) and for the finish coat. The third type, *all-purpose compound,* is used for all three coats and is by far the most popular.

No matter which variety of premixed drying-type compound you use, always start with fresh product, and seal the container securely between applications. (When you've emptied a bucket of joint compound, clean it out with water and keep it within reach. These buckets make excellent stepstools and catchalls.)

Setting-type compound comes only in powdered form. Because these products set faster and harder than drying-type compounds and better resist cracking, they are generally preferred by professionals who want to work quickly. With this type of compound, you can apply consecutive coats to the drywall in the same day. Setting time varies from ½ to 6 hours. This type also resists sanding more than drying-type compounds, so it pays to get a nice finish, or *polish*, during the application rather than depending on sanding.

Special fire-resistant joint compounds are also available (with trade names such as Fire Shield and Fire-Halt). These compounds provide fire resistance and

Preparing the Compound. *A joint compound paddle is chucked into a heavy-duty drill to mix joint compound.*

Estimating Material Quantities

Quality drywalling requires accurate estimates of material quantities. Nothing breaks your stride like having to run out to the store for materials once you've started a job. Here are some tips on how to estimate materials.

Joint Compound: You'll need roughly a gallon for every 100 square feet of gypsum drywall.

Joint Tape: To finish 500 square feet of drywall, figure on using 400 feet of tape.

Nails/Screws: This figure can vary depending on stud spacing (walls framed 16 inches on center require more fasteners than those framed at 24 inches) and on your nail or screw schedule (panels attached with adhesive require fewer fasteners). Figure on one fastener for every square foot of drywall in your job. For example, an 18 x 18-foot ceiling (324 square feet) will require about 320 screws or nails. Because one pound of 1-inch drywall screws contains about 320 screws, you'll need a pound of screws for every 320 square feet of drywall.

Drywall Panels: Estimating how much drywall you'll need to cover a room is a matter of square footage. Calculate the wall surface of the room, and divide that figure by the square footage of the panels you intend to use. For instance, a 4 x 8-foot panel measures 32 square feet. If you have a 1,000-square-foot room, you'll need just over 31 panels. Because they come in units of two, order 32 panels.

When estimating square footage, don't subtract the door or window areas (except for bay windows or unusually large doors), because you'll need extra for mistakes.

help to prevent fires from spreading through joints in walls and ceilings.

PREPARING THE COMPOUND

All joint compounds, even the premixed types, need to be stirred before use. A well-mixed compound will go on smoothly and with fewer bubbles. Mixing also ensures that the product has consistent water content throughout the entire batch.

The best accessory for mixing joint compound is a heavy-duty drill loaded with a mixing paddle. If you prefer to mix by hand (which is better for premixed joint compound), use a potato-masher-type hand mixer on a 2-foot handle. If the product is too stiff, add small amounts of water, and agitate the mixture until it is smooth enough to apply to the wall.

Finishing Wall Panels

Drywall panels are never left exposed in living areas, but not all drywall jobs require the same type of finishing—the level of drywall finish needed for a tile wall differs from the level required for a high-gloss paint finish, for example. What's best for your job? Professionals have been arguing about the proper level of finish for some time. To reach a conclusion that everyone can agree upon, four trade associations—the Gypsum Association, the Painting and Decorating Contractors of America, the Association of the Walls and Ceiling Industries International, and the Ceiling Interior Systems Construction Association—developed a consensus document called, "Recommended Levels of Gypsum Board Finish." This document spells out taping and joint compound requirements based on how the panels will be decorated. (See "Recommended Levels of Drywall Finish," page 146.)

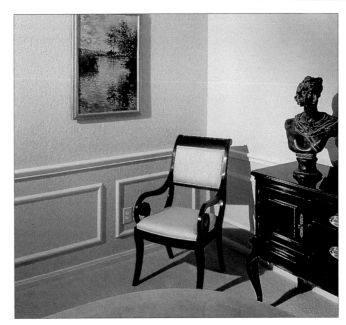

Easy Plastering. *New simpler to use plaster systems provide the looks and durability of traditional plaster systems.*

1 Drywall Basics

Drywall Options

*This is the **old-fashioned** but still workable fastening system: driving nails with a drywall hammer. (Use it very carefully because of the hatchet end.)*

*This is the **modern method** used by most pros: driving screws with a power screwdriver (or drill with a screw bit), which leaves a small dimple.*

Use a drywall corner clip *to support the panel edge when corner studs support only the adjacent sheet.*

One side of the clip *holds the panel, and the other has a tab that is nailed into the adjacent stud.*

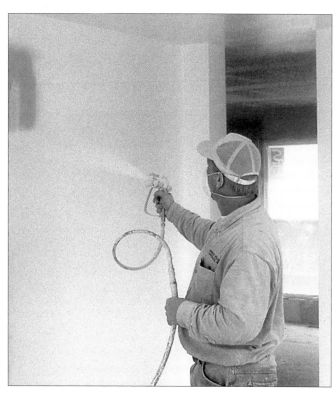

Spray-on Primers. *New primers can provide a skim-coated-type surface for paints.*

TYPICAL FINISHES

For the majority of drywall jobs, most drywallers cover the installed panels with a high-grade primer/sealer. This provides a base for finish coats of paint, and it prevents the porous panels from absorbing the top coats of paint. For high-gloss painted finishes or finishes that will be under intensive light, many professionals finish the panels with a skim coat of drywall compound before applying the primer and paint.

Special Finishes. With the popularity of decorative paint techniques and the use of glossier paint sheens on walls and ceilings, manufacturers have introduced a variety of finish products. For example, new primers developed in conjunction with drywall manufacturers provide the same finishing opportunities as a skim-coated wall. These products are designed for use in high-light areas under glossy finishes.

A number of plaster-type products provide the smoothness and durability of traditional plaster walls. The systems come in one- and two-coat varieties that expand the decorating potential of a typical drywall system. Be sure to check with the finish manufacturer to make sure the plaster-type product is compatible with the drywall panels you plan on installing.

Drywall Suspension Systems

Pre-engineered systems make installing suspended ceilings simpler than ever. Suspended ceilings are a good choice when you want to install new drywall over an old ceiling that is not level.

Using suspended ceiling technology, some systems go beyond flat ceilings, allowing for the construction of domes, ceiling vaults, and decorative soffits, opening up a range of decorative looks that was once reserved for custom-built homes or commercial buildings. Suspended ceiling systems save time and money. Interlocking components arrive on the job site ready to be fitted together. On-site fabrication of steel channels is minimal. With the exception of flat suspended ceilings, most of the newer ceiling systems are best left to professionals. Many are custom-built based on an architect's plans. (For more information see, "Suspended Ceilings," pages 58-62.)

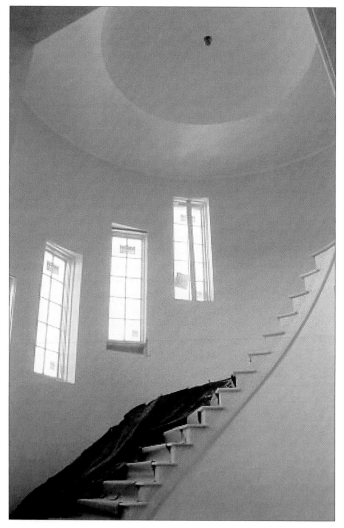

Domes, Arches, Deep Soffits. *New Suspended ceiling systems make possible a range of decorative possibilities.*

Chapter 2

Tools & Equipment

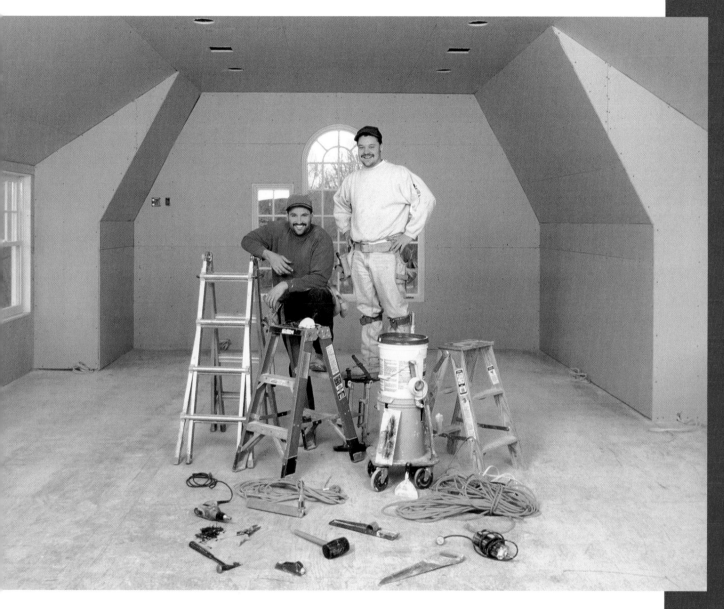

Any drywall job, large or small, requires four kinds of tools and equipment: safety equipment to protect eyes and lungs; marking and cutting instruments that ensure precise lengths, angles, and holes; hanging tools to position and fasten panels; and finishing equipment to apply joint compound and sand seams.

As with other facets of residential construction, the tools and equipment for drywalling have improved over the years. Panel jacks make hanging ceilings easier by eliminating the need to balance panels on your head. Strap-on stilts can save a thousand ladder or scaffold moves. A tape bender and cornering tools can save hours of sanding corner seams, and modern dust barriers help contain a job's mess. You may not need every tool and accessory described in this chapter for every job, but it helps to know the available options before you dive into your next project.

Personal Safety Tools

Gypsum drywall and the products used to install and finish it generally contain no toxic substances. However, the dominant by-product of installation, referred to by NIOSH and OSHA as *nuisance dust*, will irritate your eyes and lungs. To save yourself unnecessary aggravation, wear protective gear, especially when sawing and sanding.

Because gypsum dust is just a nuisance and not hazardous, you can get by with one of the disposable **dust masks,** especially if you're not allergic or otherwise sensitive to the dust. You can also use one of the NIOSH- or OSHA-approved nuisance-dust masks, also called **dust/mist respirators.** The best of these have a reinforced molded shell and an exhaust valve.

Safety glasses are useful for installing and finishing drywall. During installation, when you're cutting panels with a utility knife and driving screws with a screw gun or drill, you put your eyes at risk. When hanging ceiling panels, you face the hazard of falling grit, and it's easy to flick a drop of joint compound into your eye during finish work. Look for NIOSH- or OSHA-approved clear plastic glasses with side protectors, and steer clear of goggles, which can fog up.

Hoisting and positioning panels may hyperextend the lower back, so it's a good idea to wear a **lower-back support** even if you don't have back problems. The best type of support is a stave-reinforced, breathable nylon back brace, which wraps around your lower back, upper buttocks, and abdomen. It should have two outer elastic bands that pull tight for a snug fit.

When positioning panels on a ceiling, you'll need both hands to load and drive screws with your drill. It sounds odd, but drywallers commonly use their heads to hold panels in place. If you have a construction **hardhat** or light helmet in your basement, use it during this part of the operation. Tape a sponge on top of the helmet, both to protect the panel and relieve strain on your head.

Although moving panels is a two-man job, one person can carry an 8-foot panel with the aid of a **panel carrier.** This tool hooks under one edge of the panel, giving you a handle to hold the bottom without hurting your fingers and allowing you to hold on to the other edge of the panel at shoulder level.

Dust Mask. Important when cutting drywall and sanding joints, a dust mask protects the lungs from the irritating dust created by powdered gypsum and joint compound.

Dust-Mist Respirator. You can buy changeable filters for a respirator if you're particularly sensitive to dust.

Safety Glasses. Eye protection is recommended when installing drywall, especially when working on a ceiling. Chunks of crumbling drywall and dust can fall into your eyes, causing severe irritation and possibly permanent damage.

Lower-Back Support. This harness is desirable when lifting and manipulating drywall panels, which can weigh 45 to 70 lbs. each.

Hardhat. This can be useful to protect your head while holding up ceiling panels—provided you add a sponge on top to protect the panel.

Panel Carrier. One person can easily carry 8-ft. drywall panels by hooking a carrier onto one edge of the panel. To prevent back injury, avoid quick movements as you rise to a standing position.

Keeping the Worksite Clean

Drywalling creates dust. Even if you use a dust-free sanding method (such as a dampened sanding sponge), cutting and installing the panels is dusty work. Dust control is a major concern, especially if you're remodeling part of a finished house. Dust will drift invisibly through open doorways, or even underneath a closed door, and you'll find it settled on every surface in your home. This situation calls for a dust curtain over each doorway or wall area that opens into an occupied room and floor protection for any finished area that you are likely to traverse. You should also vacuum the site at the end of each work day.

You'll also find some fairly sophisticated dust-control equipment on the market today, called curtain wall, or dust door and wall systems. These products consist of frames that are erected in doorways or open areas, which seal plastic against walls without using tape or nails. There are doorways in the plastic, which can be zippered open and shut.

Unfortunately, these systems cost money. You can make a perfectly adequate dust control system using furring strips, duct tape, and 6-mil polyethylene plastic (the kind sold as painter's dropcloth). Trap a sheet of plastic against an unfinished wall over a door opening with furring strips, and then screw through the furring and plastic sheet into the wall. If you will need to use a doorway and can't block it off, slit the plastic wall down the center, and drape a wide plastic curtain over the slit. For improved dust protection, create an "airlock" by installing two of these plastic walls in tandem 3 feet apart. To protect carpet and flooring, roll out 6-mil plastic and duct-tape it to the floor.

Furring Strips

6-mil poly

Dust Barrier. Although you can buy commercial barriers with zippers, you can also make one using furring and 6-mil polyethylene. Tack a piece of plastic in a doorway, and slit an opening in its center. Drape another piece over it, which will act as a door.

Measuring & Marking Tools

A quality job starts with exact measurements. Marking your panels accurately is crucial to good installation. The handiest tool you'll use is a **measuring tape.** Look for a 25-foot locking steel tape with a 1-inch-wide blade. (The wide blade stays rigid out to approximately 7 feet, which makes it useful when one person is measuring something out of reach.)

You'll also need a **chalk-line box** for snapping cut lines on panels. This tool consists of nothing more than a long piece of heavy cotton twine covered with chalk dust (usually blue) that reels in and out of a box. The twine has a clip at one end that hooks onto the panel edge. When you pull the line taut and snap it, it leaves a perfectly straight mark, which usually won't show through paint like a pencil line.

Drywalling doesn't require many highly specialized tools; before starting a project, make sure you have the basics on hand.

Measuring Tape. *A self-retracting tape is an essential tool for making long measurements, such as along lengthy walls.*

Chalk-Line Box. *This tool is handy when cutting long lengths of drywall panels. "Snapping a line" is often the only way to get a long, clean, straight cut line.*

Pencils. *You should always have pencils available and already sharpened.*

Claw Hammer. *This common tool is good to have for quick framing changes and alterations.*

Pliers. *This is a good tool to have for a quick scaffolding fix and general repairs.*

Screwdrivers. *Phillips-head and flat-blade screwdrivers are essential for simple mechanical and electrical repairs and adjustments.*

Level. *A 4-ft. spirit level is often called for when drywalling. Setting a panel with plumb edges is essential, especially when it will be used as a reference to set subsequent panels in a series.*

A standard **framing square** is essential for marking straight lines, clean corners, and accurate 45-degree angles. You'll find that a 4-foot aluminum **T-square** is indispensable for any drywalling job. This tool lets you draw perfectly square lines across the entire width of a standard panel, and the rule marks stenciled on the tongue and blade allow exact positioning of smaller measurements. Keep a **combination square** handy, as well, for marking short lines perfectly on the square. A carpenter's **spirit level,** preferably 4 feet long, comes in handy for positioning panels and furring, and it makes a good straightedge for drawing longer lines.

If you have out-of-plumb walls or are butting drywall to masonry, you'll need a **compass,** or scriber. This ordinary marking tool is used to fit the edge of a panel to any irregular adjoining edge or surface. Run one arm of the compass down an out-of-plumb wall, and the other (pencil-loaded) arm copies a line onto the panel, allowing you to achieve an exact fit.

Besides the tools mentioned above, keep some of the standard hand tools close by, including a **hammer,** several **screwdrivers,** a pair of **pliers,** and a **chisel.** You'll use these to adjust tools and equipment, open joint-compound buckets, and repair scaffolding.

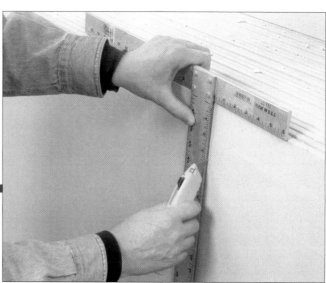

An aluminum T-square, available in any hardware store, helps making straight cuts on drywall a quick, clean job.

2 Tools & Equipment

4-ft. T-square. This is a helpful tool for making clean square cuts on drywall panels. By placing the T-square in position and using it to guide a utility knife, you can skip the step of marking cut lines with a pencil and freehand the cuts.

Combination Square. You'll find this a handy tool to have on hand for making shorter square and angled cuts in drywall panels, as well as a marking tool for some long, straight cuts.

Compass. Also called a scriber, it enables you to copy the irregular contour of an out-of-plumb or masonry wall.

Tool Belt. This is a useful item for carrying screws, nails, and hand tools.

Framing Square. This tool is useful for many measuring and cutting tasks, such as checking framing for square.

Hanging & Cutting Tools

A **drywall hammer,** also called a convex-headed, bevel-headed, or bell-faced hammer, is an ideal tool for drywalling, even if you are using screws as fasteners. The crosshatched convex head leaves a dimple that fills in neatly with joint compound. You're less likely to tear the panels' face paper with this tool, and its tapered opposite end can be used for wedging and prying panels.

When it comes to driving screws, a battery-powered **cordless drill** with a magnetic drive bit offers the most convenience. You can also buy one of several **drywalling screw guns,** which are drills designed especially for this task. They have a magnetic bit to hold the screw and an adjustable clutch that ensures consistent screwhead depth. These screw guns can be fitted with an attachment that feeds a plastic band of collated screws into the drill bit, so you don't have to fish around in your pouch every time you need a screw. If you are doing a lot of drywalling, this tool will pay for itself in short order.

A **drywall saw** has extra-coarse teeth and a short blade that make it perfect for trimming excess drywall around door and window frames. A **utility saw,** which has a pointed, knife-like blade and finer teeth than a drywall saw, comes in handy for cutting out holes for utility boxes, pipes, and ductwork. To start the cut, you thrust the pointed blade tip through the drywall. And don't forget a **utility knife.** Buy the retractable type, and get plenty of extra blades to ensure clean cuts.

A **surface-forming rasp** is a tool used for shaving edges. It resembles a plane from the top, but has a rough grating blade underneath that files down drywall quickly. You'd use one to remove $1/8$ inch or less of material (for example, to fit a panel against a protruding framing member) or to clean up a jagged edge left by a dull utility knife.

Drywall Saw. *This saw is good for cutting out door and window openings and trimming excess.*

Drywall Hammer.
This special hammer is designed to drive nails and leave a dimple behind around the nailhead. The hammer has a symmetrical convex face for this purpose. The dull tapered blade is for levering and fine-tuning panel position.

Drywalling Screw Gun.
Load a screw into the bit of this special tool, designed just for driving drywall screws, and when the screw is driven to the proper depth, a clutch will disengage the bit, leaving the screw just below the surface of the drywall's face.

Cordless Drill. *With the addition of a special clutch, this is a handy tool for driving drywall screws. Get two batteries: one to use as a second one charges.*

Utility Knife. *This is the tool most often used to cut drywall panels. Be sure it is loaded with a fresh, sharp razor blade, otherwise it will tear the face paper as it cuts.*

Surface-Forming Rasp. *Use this device to shave off small amounts of drywall along the edges of the panels. It's a handy tool to have if you have cut your drywall panel just a hair too long.*

A **drywall ripper** proves useful for cutting narrow strips of stock to fit into tight corners next to window and door frames or just for trimming a few inches off a panel. It has twin blades that can be set to an exact width. By butting the ripper against the edge of a panel and drawing it along the face, you make two parallel cuts that allow you to snap off the strip cleanly.

When fitted with the proper bit or blade, routers, saber saws, and other **power cutting tools** (such as Porter-Cable's Cutout Tool or Hyde's Roto-Zip) make for quick and accurate drywall cutting. However, you're better off avoiding these tools unless you have effective dust-collection equipment.

A **circle cutter,** also called a hole compass, lets you measure and cut circular holes for pipes, lighting fixtures, and utility boxes. It has a center rod through which slides a locking L-shape arm that adjusts to the radius of your circle. The end of the arm has a cutting edge that rotates around the axis of the center rod, cutting into the drywall.

A **caulking gun** is necessary if you plan to attach your panels with an adhesive. Simply load the gun with a tube of adhesive, and a plate attached to a ratcheting arm forces the adhesive out through the tube's nozzle, which you trim to produce the desired size and shape of bead. Note: if you're installing a double layer of panels for sound-deadening purposes, adhesive is essential.

A **panel lifter** (also called a foot jig) looks like a miniature seesaw. By slipping the thin-lipped front end of the jig beneath a drywall panel and stepping on the back end, you can lift the panel 2 or 3 inches. You can buy a panel lifter or make one in the shop from a pair of 3-inch-wide lengths of pine. Trim one end of the pieces to a thickness that will fit under (but still support) a panel. In a pinch, you can use a pry bar and block of wood for this purpose.

Drywall Ripper. This tool has two opposing blades that spin around a pin-pointed center axis. This tool is handy for trimming strips less than 5 in. wide.

Utility Saw. This is the ideal tool for poking through in the middle of a piece of drywall and cutting out small holes for utility boxes, pipes, and ducts.

Aviation Snips. A high-quality pair of snips is needed to cut various metal and plastic corner beads and edgings to size.

Power Cutting Tool. A cutout tool can save a lot of time making holes, but it also raises a lot of dust. Pros generally use this tool to cut around electrical outlets and fixtures, such as recessed lighting.

Circle Cutter. The wheel blade on this device spins around a pin-pointed center axis. The arm on which the blade is mounted is adjustable, so the tool can cut circles of various diameters.

Caulking Gun. This is the best way to apply adhesive to studs.

Panel Lifter. This lever is slipped beneath the bottom edge of a piece of drywall. When you press down on the back end of the panel lifter, the drywall can be lifted up 2 in. or so, for fine-tuning its placement.

Finishing Tools

TAPING KNIVES

To apply tape and joint compound, you'll need taping (or finishing) knives. These come in four or five different styles, each designed for a specific task. New knives often are coated with a rust-preventive sealant, which you'll need to sand off before use. After each job, make sure you clean your knives carefully in warm water and dry them to prevent rusting: a rusty knife can play havoc with finish work. Disposable plastic knives are also available.

Use a **2- or 3-inch knife** to apply joint compound in tight spots—for example, where a door jamb nearly

meets a corner. This knife doesn't have many other uses, but you don't want to be caught without one should the need arise. The multipurpose **5- or 6-inch knife** will prove to be your most versatile tool. Use it to press tape into the bedding compound, to cover the tape with the second layer, and to cover voids left by fastener heads.

When applying wide coats of joint compound, you'll want the widest knife you can properly control. A **12- to 16-inch finishing trowel,** which resembles a mason's trowel, works best for this purpose. This tool should have a slight curve so that it leaves a barely perceptible crown in the center of the coat.

The **12-inch straight-handled knife,** a larger version of the versatile 6-inch tool, has a handle that extends across the base of the blade. This adds rigidity, making it ideal for feathering out wide joint-compound seams.

The 6-in. taping knife will be in your hand more than any other drywall tool—spend a little more to get the highest quality.

2- to 3-in. Knife. These small knives are the tools for applying joint compound in tight spaces, like the area between a corner door frame and a wall, where larger knives won't fit.

5- or 6-in. Knife. This is the tool that gets the most use on all drywall jobs. It is great for applying joint compound and for scooping fresh joint compound out of a bucket.

Two-Faced Corner Knife. This knife can help leave a professional finish on joint compound in corners, though it takes practice to master.

12-in. Straight-Handled Knife. This drywall knife is required for applying wider coats of joint compound. Having one on site is an absolute must.

12- to 16-in. Finishing Trowel. Use this trowel to smooth coats of joint compound. Its long blade enables you to leave a wide, consistent finish while keeping blade marks to a minimum.

A **corner knife** is used to finish inside corner seams. It has two faces, each about 3 inches square, that meet at a slightly pointed corner, with a handle like a regular taping knife.

OTHER FINISHING TOOLS

A **hawk** consists of a flat panel of aluminum, anywhere from 8 to 14 inches square (but usually about 12 inches), with a short handle mounted on its back face. It simply provides a convenient way to hold joint compound when you're taping a room, so you needn't keep running back to the bucket. The top may have grooves that keep the joint compound from sliding off.

A **mud tray,** much like a wallpaper-pasting tray, can also be used to carry joint compound easily from place to place. If you don't want to buy a hawk, these plastic trays are just as handy, being light enough to hold in one hand.

Sandpaper (120-grit or finer) is used to take down burrs, ridges, and high spots between coats and to finish off top coats. To streamline this job, you can use a **hand sander** or **pole sander.** These tools have a plate that accepts a half-sheet of sandpaper. The pole has a universal joint attached to the plate. After applying the top coat, go over the seams with a sander to smooth them out. Some sandpaper comes in precut half-lengths for use with these tools.

Polyurethane sponges offer an excellent and nearly dust-free way to smooth joint compound. These sponges come in various grits, but stick with 120-grit or finer for drywall finishing. Dampen the sponge before use, and be careful to squeeze out all excess water between passes.

A **tape dispenser,** worn on your belt, frees up your hands to do taping work while feeding you the tape. You load the roll onto a drum that rotates on a belt

Mud Trays.
Trays such as these, which can be held in one hand, allow you to carry small amounts of compound with you as you finish a room.

Tape Dispenser.
Hung from your belt, this is a convenient way to dispense paper tape while working.

Hawk. *A hawk allows you to carry wet joint compound with you as you finish joints and fastener-head voids.*

Polyurethane Sponge. *A small-celled sponge offers a dust-free alternative to sanding. It is ideal in areas that can tolerate no dust, like an office or a finished area that requires only a single wall or patch installed.*

Hand Sander. *This is a practical, easy way to sand walls and ceilings. Load it with half sheets of 120-grit sandpaper.*

Sanding Pole. *A long pole wiith a universal joint is a convenient and simple way to sand walls and ceilings. Load it with 120-grit sandpaper.*

clip. A feed mechanism can automatically fold the tape if desired.

Shoe stilts strap onto your shoes and calves, giving you an extra 18 to 24 inches of height and thereby eliminating the need for scaffolding or ladders. They save a great deal of time and effort, but can be difficult to use and are not permitted by all safety codes.

A **panel jack** or panel lift can save you a lot of backwork during ceiling installation, especially if you're working alone. An adjustable metal frame that cradles the panel can be raised or lowered by cranking a handle. The entire jack is mounted on casters and maneuvers easily. Raise the panel into place, and the panel jack holds it snugly until you've secured it. This device also works well for mounting panels high on tall walls.

A **deadman,** also called a T-brace or T-support, is a handy accessory you can make in the shop from furring strips or scrap stock. Make the top member of the T about 3 feet long, and the post about an inch longer than the distance from floor to ceiling. (In other words, make it approximately 8 feet 1 inch long for an 8-foot ceiling.) You wedge the deadman beneath a ceiling panel, pinning it in place for screwing or nailing. The top piece of the deadman should be covered with a piece of foam or scrap of carpet to protect the ceiling from damage.

Gaining Height

On most drywall jobs, you will need to place drywall panels with the aid of a ladder, bench, or scaffold—something to provide you and your helper with the extra height to reach the work area. Stepladders work well enough for small jobs, but if you are drywalling an entire room, the act of installing a panel and then moving two ladders so that you and a helper can lift the next panel into position will slow you down. For large jobs, consider using a rolling scaffold. The scaffold allows you and a helper to work at a comfortable height and the scaffold is easy to move. Working on a scaffold is safer than trying to keep your balance on a stepladder while handling drywall panels. (For more on rolling scaffolds, see "Using a Scaffold," page 79.)

Pros own their own scaffolds, but you can rent one from a tool rental shop. Be sure you ask about assembly before leaving the rental agency.

Panel Jack. *This will save a lot of labor when working on ceilings or high walls. Panels are singly loaded onto a frame, which can be raised and lowered with a crank. Wheels allow for exact positioning.*

Shoe Stilts. *These stilts allow you to work on a ceiling and the higher parts of a wall without having to move ladders or scaffolding. They take getting used to and should be used with great care.*

BUILDING A DEADMAN

A deadman is a brace that allows you to install ceiling panels while working alone. This site-built tool is made using 2×4s that are fashioned into a reinforced T-shape. The overall height of the deadman should be high enough to allow you to wedge the deadman under the ceiling panel. However, if the fit is too tight, you many damage the panel. Another option is to build the deadman about 2 inches short of the actual ceiling height. At that height, the panel will rest just below the ceiling joists when you lift it into position, allowing you to push the panel into place against the joist with one hand while you attach the panel with the other hand.

Make the crosspiece about 3 feet long to provide adequate support across the width of the panels. To protect the drywall, attach scrap carpeting or foam to the top of the crosspiece. Add reinforcement by nailing angle braces as shown below. It is also a good idea to attach a section of rubber hose to the bottom of the vertical support to keep the deadman from slipping on the floor.

To use the deadman, attach a temporary nailer to support one end of the sheet. Lift the sheet into position, and apply pressure with the deadman. Be sure to keep the crosspiece under a ceiling joist. Don't apply pressure to an unsupported section of drywall.

1. *Build a basic T-shape support out of 2x4s. Overall height should be about 2 in. short of the ceiling.*

2. *Keep the main support from wobbling by attaching angle braces of 2x4s or lighter wood.*

3. *Attach a temporary nailer to support one end of the sheet while you raise the other with the deadman.*

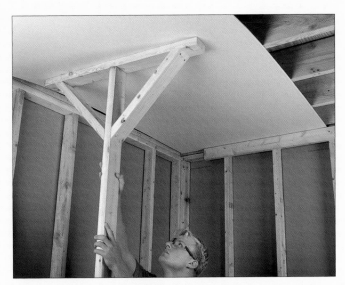

4. *Use the deadman for support, but keep applying pressure to prevent the panel from slipping off the nailer.*

MECHANICAL FINISHING TOOLS

Mechanical tools can speed the taping and finishing process. Most tool sets contain a basic applicator with interchangeable heads to complete different phases of the taping process.

The basic taping tool applies the tape and a thin layer of joint compound in one pass. Most are designed to completely fill the tapered seam between drywall panels. Other tools apply wider layers of compound to complete the seam taping process just as you would when finishing by hand. There are also tools to tape and apply joint compound to inside and outside corners, and special tools to fill fastener indentations with joint compound.

With some models, joint compound is loaded into the tool and then squeezed out during application. Other tools are pneumatically driven, using air to pump joint compound from a reservoir. Better types of tools allow you to adjust the flow rate so that you can apply joint compound to suit your needs.

Mechanical tools have a number of advantages over hand taping. Once you have mastered the tools, you will find you achieve consistent results. The work

Angled Heads. *Mechanical tapers with angled heads allow you to complete vertical seams easily.*

will go quicker and there will be less sanding at the end of the project than is usually necessary with hand finishing drywall seams.

The downside to automatic tools is that they are expensive. Unless you plan on drywalling an entire house, it is probably best to stick with hand tools. Mechanical applicators also take some time to learn how to use correctly. Some professionals send their crews to classes conducted by the tool manufacturer. To keep the tools operating effectively, you will need to closely follow instructions for cleanup. And even if you do use mechanical tapers, most jobs will still require some hand finishing.

Finishing Corners. *This tool contains small tabs that convert a coater to a tool for finishing corner bead.*

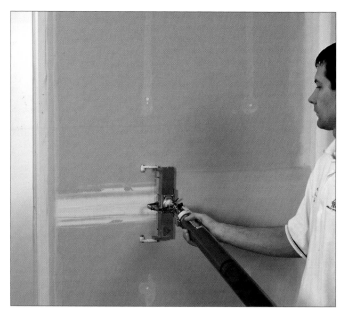

Tapered Seams. *By switching coater heads you can apply wider layers of joint compound to finish tapered seams.*

Chapter 3

Wall & Ceiling Prep

You can't overstate the importance of carefully preparing a wall or ceiling for dry-walling. Because the panels measure only $1/2$ inch or so thick, they roughly contour the framing members or other surface to which they're fastened. Any irregularity, such as an out-of-plumb-on-the-face or protruding stud or joist, will show through the drywall panel once it's up. To prevent unpleasant surprises, you need to know how to locate and correct these irregularities before they compromise your drywalling job.

*B*efore preparing the walls and ceilings, you'll want to create a layout plan that uses as many full panels (4 × 8 feet or longer) as possible. Fewer joints make for less mess, less waste, and less taping work (which accounts for most of the man-hours in any drywalling project). This chapter will offer some strategies for reducing panel usage and a few common framing practices that make it easier to use your materials to the best advantage.

Laying Out a Drywall Job

Drywalling may well rank first among the most wasteful of the construction trades, partly because the material is relatively inexpensive. Trimming a 4 × 8-foot panel to fit a 3 × 6-foot space leaves you with odd-shaped cutoffs that can't be used elsewhere. Ideally, you would install a single piece of custom-fitted drywall large enough to cover an entire wall. Because that's impossible in most cases, you go with the largest pieces you can handle. This invariably means cutting large sheets down to size—you never want to patch together smaller pieces to fill out a wall. If some waste occurs along the way (and it will), that's the price of doing a clean, professional job.

Keep in mind the following three objectives when laying out any drywall job:

◾ Minimize the number of joints by using the smallest number of the largest panels that will fit in your room.

◾ Avoid end-butted flush joints, which usually require joining two untapered panel ends (the most difficult joints to finish).

◾ Set up the layout for ease of installation by eliminating multiple moves of wallboard stacks, ladders, scaffolding, and so on.

GETTING THE MOST OUT OF YOUR MATERIALS
The following schematics show typical horizontal installations for 10-, 16-, and 20-foot-long walls. Notice in each case that a bit of planning can reduce the number of panels required and the occurrence of end-butted joints. Note also how the various layouts affect the linear footage of joints that need finishing.

THE 10-FOOT WALL
Layout number 1 uses three 4 × 8-foot panels rather inefficiently. The resulting installation leaves you with a 2 × 8-foot cutoff and a long end-butted flush joint. You end up with a total of 16 linear feet of joint to tape and finish.

Layout number 2 shows two 4 × 10-foot panels installed horizontally. This, the recommended installation, yields no cutoffs, no end-butted flush joint, and only 10 linear feet of taping and finishing work.

Layout No. 1

This 10 x 8-ft. wall layout uses two and one-half 8-ft. drywall panels and has 16 lin. ft. of joint, including an 8-ft. end-butted flush joint. It can be improved upon using longer panels.

Layout No. 2

This 10 x 8-ft. wall layout uses just two 10-ft. drywall panels and creates just 10 lin. ft. of joint with no end-butt flush joint. This layout is an improvement on the layout shown in the above illustration.

THE 16-FOOT WALL

Of the four alternatives presented here, only numbers 2 and 4 eliminate end-butt flush joints, and of those two, the fourth (and recommended) installation leaves fewer linear feet of finish work.

Layout number 1 shows two 4 × 12-foot panels installed horizontally, with an 8-foot-long panel installed vertically at one end. This leaves you with 20 linear feet of joint to finish, including an end-butt joint.

Layout number 2 uses four 8-foot panels installed vertically. This eliminates end-butt joints, but you have 24 linear feet of joint to finish. Note that vertical seams are more difficult to finish than horizontal joints.

In layout number 3, you have four panels to install and an end-butt joint to finish. You also end up with 24 linear feet of joint overall.

Layout number 4, the recommended one, calls for just two 4 × 16-foot panels. This installation leaves you with no wasted wallboard, no end-butt flush joints, and just 16 linear feet of taping and finishing work.

The Pros Know

If you're only using 8-foot panels, a quick way to estimate the number you'll need for the walls is to measure the perimeter of the room and divide this by 4 (rounding up fractions). Deduct about ¼ sheet for windows, ⅓ sheet for doors, and ⅔ sheet for sliding glass doors or bay windows.

Layout No. 1

This 16 x 8-ft. wall layout is inefficient, as it uses two 12-ft. panels and an 8-ft. panel in a configuration that creates an end-butt joint and a total of 20 lin. ft. of joint. It can be improved upon.

Layout No. 2

This 16 x 8-ft. wall layout creates 24 lin. ft. of joint, but there are no end-butt joints, and that's a good tradeoff for the higher linear feet. Though this layout is an improvement on the one shown above, it is not optimal.

Layout No. 3

This 16 x 8-ft. wall layout creates a total of 24 lin. ft. of joint, including an 8-ft. end-butt joint. Worse, the butt joint comes at the center of the wall, where it will draw attention to itself.

Layout No. 4

This 16 x 8-ft. wall layout creates no butt joints and only 16 lin. ft. of joint to tape and finish. Of the three other 16-ft. wall layouts shown here, this is the optimal strategy.

Layout No. 1

End-Butt Joints

4'

8'

4'   8'   8'

20'

This layout for a wall measuring 20 x 8 ft. uses six 4 x 8-ft. panels. It creates 36 lin. ft. of joint, including two end-butt joints. It can be improved upon using larger panels.

Layout No. 2

End-Butt Joint

4'

8'

10'   10'

20'

This 20 x 8-ft. wall layout uses four 10-ft. drywall panels. It creates 28 lin. ft. of joint including an end-butt joint. Unfortunately, the butt joint is right at the center of the wall, where it will be most noticeable.

Layout No. 3

End-Butt Joint

4'

8'

4'   16'

20'

Though it has only 24 lin. ft. of joint, this 20 x 8-ft. wall layout has an end-butt joint. This end-butt joint is long and may call attention to itself.

Layout No. 4

16'

End-Butt Joint

4'

8'

End-Butt Joint

4'   16'

20'

This 20 x 8-ft. layout is acceptable because it uses the longest panels available, yet where end-butt joints are unavoidable, it staggers them so that they won't call attention to themselves.

Layout No. 5

8'

4'   4'   4'   4'   4'

20'

Using 5 vertical 8-ft. panels, this 20 x 8-ft. layout eliminates end-butt joints but leaves you with 32 lin. ft. of floor-to-ceiling joints.

THE 20-FOOT WALL

Of the five layouts shown here, one eliminates end-butt joints and one places short-end butt joints near either end of the wall in staggered fashion, which makes them less noticeable. Both are recommended because they present trade-offs between end-butt joints and longer tapered joints.

Layout number 1 shows four 8-foot and two 4-foot panels installed horizontally. This installation yields two end-butt flush joints and a total of 36 linear feet of joint to finish. Although it creates no waste, it requires you to handle six individual pieces of drywall.

In layout number 2, four 10-foot-long panels create an end-butt joint in the most noticeable location—dead-center on the wall, running from floor to ceiling. This leaves you with only 28 linear feet of joint to finish, but the unfortunate placement of the end-butt joint outweighs this advantage.

Layout number 3 calls for just three panels and yields a mere 24 linear feet of finishing work. Unfortunately, you end up with an obvious floor-to-ceiling end-butt joint.

In layout number 4, a recommended installation, you use a pair of 16-foot panels plus two 4-foot pieces to fill in the remaining areas. This solution avoids the continuous floor-to-ceiling end-butt joint by staggering the two long panels. You still have two 4-foot end-butt joints to finish, but this layout places them near each end of the wall, where they attract less attention. Overall, this installation requires just 28 linear feet of finish work, a substantial improvement over the 36 linear feet of layout number 1.

Layout number 5 shows five 8-foot panels installed vertically with no end-butt joints, which is why it is recommended. However, this layout leaves you with 32 feet of joint to finish.

Framing Tips for Drywall

FRAMING DIMENSIONS AND DRYWALL

Drywall comes in a standard 48-inch width because most framing codes require either a 16- or 24-inch on-center framing schedule. Whichever schedule is used, a 48-inch-wide panel installed parallel with studs or joists should end centered on a framing member.

For this reason, it's critical that you work with accurately framed studs and joists. Each pair of adjoining panels must normally share a two-by that measures only 1½ inches wide. If a framing member is misaligned by as little as ½ inch, it can throw off your drywalling, because standard-sized panels won't have proper anchor points along their edges for nails or screws.

INSTALLING NAILER BLOCKS

Builders often install top wall plates (the horizontal 2×4s or 2×6s that cap stud-framed walls) directly under ceiling joists. This can lead to problems later

Framing Tips for Drywall. *Check—and mark—joists and studs to be sure all panels have sufficient bearing. Also check for crooked, misaligned, or loose studs before you begin drywalling.*

The Pros Know

When you install drywall on a ceiling, you can orient panels either perpendicular or parallel to the ceiling joists. Neither approach makes taping the joints any easier, but panels will sag less if installed across the joists rather than aligned with them lengthwise.

On walls, horizontal orientation may not only reduce the linear seam footage, but it can also make taping easier. Because the joint falls approximately at waist level, you don't have to reach overhead to finish the top half of every panel.

2x4 Stud Wall
16" O.C.

2x4 Stud Wall
24" O.C.

Framing Dimensions and Drywall. *Walls framed 16 in. on center (the most common stud-to-stud distance) will offer superior backing to vertical drywall panels, with two studs supporting the interior of the panel and one on each edge. Walls framed at 24 in. on center (found in older homes) offer only one stud to support the center of the panel and one on each edge.*

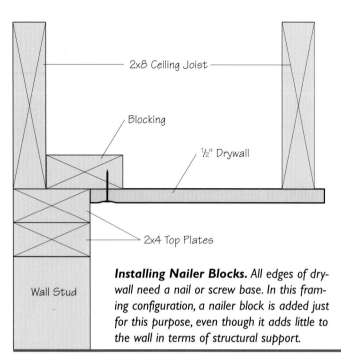

Installing Nailer Blocks. *All edges of drywall need a nail or screw base. In this framing configuration, a nailer block is added just for this purpose, even though it adds little to the wall in terms of structural support.*

Backing Joints and Edges. *When hanging thin (³/₈-in. or less) drywall horizontally, one edge of the panel may not have backing between studs (left). This could lead to cracking over time. In this situation, blocking should be added in each stud bay to accommodate the thinner panels (right).*

because it provides no fastening base (or lip) for the edge of ceiling drywall. Without backing, the panel edge joint can crack over time—sometimes even when pressure is applied during painting. To add a fastening base, install a block that runs the full length of the top plate and extends half of its width beyond the top plate's inside edge. When installing panels, nail or screw them to this blocking as you would to any stud or joist.

BACKING JOINTS AND EDGES

Optimally, panel edges should be fastened flush against framing members, whether they be furring strips, pieces of blocking, studs, or top/bottom plates. However, in some situations—for example, where drywall is installed horizontally on stud-framed walls or ceiling joists—nonbacked edges will bridge stud or joist bays. In these cases, you'll want 16-inch-on-center framing in order to reduce as much as possible the span between studs.

Of course, a remodeling job gives you no control over the existing framing, and you may be forced to drywall over 24-inch-on-center studs. If this is the case, and you're installing thinner (³/₈-inch) panels, you'll need to install horizontal blocking between the stud bays. If you can't install blocking, either orient the drywall vertically or use thicker panels.

When installing full-length panels, you may be tempted to position two flush ends so that they meet in the middle of a stud bay. However, this would leave the end-butt joint unbacked, making it vulner-

able to any slight pressure. To save yourself messy repair work later on, always back joints with a stud or furring strip, even though this often requires trimming the panel to length. The same holds true for tapered edges. These long edges should always rest flush against, and be fastened to, some part of the framing, either furring strips, studs, or top plates.

STAGGERING END-BUTT JOINTS

In many drywall jobs, you can't avoid creating end-butted joints (between untapered panel ends). This is especially true in long runs on walls or ceilings.

Staggering End-Butt Joints. *When installing drywall panels on a wall or ceiling, stagger the end-butt flush joints as shown here. When end-butt seams are lined up, they call attention to themselves.*

Checking and Correcting Alignment. *Check the alignment of surfaces you will finish—drywall reflects any flaws in the supporting framing.*

Because end-butt joints make for difficult finish work and tend to draw attention to themselves (even when neatly finished), it's best not to align them on adjacent rows of drywall. If you must have end-butt joints, try to place them opposite each other near the ends of a wall. On ceilings or walls with long runs, start your first row of drywall with a half panel, the second row with a full panel, and so on, much the way a house is stagger-sheathed with plywood.

Checking & Correcting Alignment

With today's declining lumber quality, more and more studs are bowed, cupped, or twisted. This can create problems for the drywaller, who depends on precise, predictable spacing between studs. In addition, every piece of framing should lie in the same plane so that drywall panels will hang perfectly flat.

Inconsistency in the framing caused by bowed studs and misalignment will be broadcast through the drywall as wavy walls or bulges for all to see in the finished job.

If part of a built-up ceiling beam or corner post protrudes, the panel must ride over this obstruction and will likely crack when you nail it home from the other side. If you can't pound down the obstruction with a framing hammer, use a surface-forming rasp to carve a shallow seat for the obstruction in the back of the drywall.

DETECTING A MISALIGNED STUD

Tools and Materials

Difficulty Level:

- ◼ Measuring tape
- ◼ Three identical standoff blocks
- ◼ Three 10d nails or drywall screws
- ◼ Sturdy string as long as the wall
- ◼ Hammer or cordless screw gun

1. INSTALL BLOCKS.

Attach one block at each end of the stud wall. Also partially attach a fastener to the side of the block. The blocks should be at the same height.

2. TIE ON STRING.

Tie a string to the fasteners so that it stands off the stud wall a distance equal to the depth of the blocks.

3. CHECK FOR LEVEL PLANE.

Try to slide the third block beneath the string. If studs are bowed outward, the string will impede the block, and you'll have to stretch the string to get it around the block. If studs are bowed inward, there will be a space between the block and the string. Check every stud in your wall.

4. CHECK ON-CENTER STUD SPACING.

Use a measuring tape to make sure that the on-center spacing is consistent from stud to stud. Keep in mind that some studs must provide anchorage for two panels, so the on-center distance should come close to the center of those studs, no more than $\frac{1}{4}$ inch out of alignment. Correct a misplaced stud by withdrawing the nails, repositioning the stud, and renailing it in its proper location.

1. *Check to see if a wall is straight by using the string-and-block standoff method. Use three blocks the same size. Set one on each end of the wall with a string between them.*

Tie off.

2. *Tie off the string at one end, and then pulling the string taut, loop the string several times around the other screw. This will capture the string and keep it from slipping.*

3. *The gap or the bow between the string and the block will demonstrate the relationship of the stud to the rest of the wall.*

4. *Before drywalling, check to make sure the on-center distance between studs is consistent. Once the drywall is in place and hiding the studs, you will use the on-center spacing to guide the placement of fasteners.*

Adding a Niche

Popular at the turn of the century, wall niches faded away as homes became less fancy during the postwar housing boom. Although an Italian marble niche deep enough to hold a statue is going to be an expensive proposition, a simple shallow niche made from drywall or even preformed dense polyurethane is an easy addition to any partition wall, even if you haven't planned ahead for it in your framing.

It's unwise to put a niche into an exterior wall, as you'll lose insulation at that spot. The depth of your niche will be limited, then, by the depth of the partition wall (generally 3½ inches, the width of a 2x4)—although a shelf on the bottom could extend the depth enough to hold a telephone or larger vase. It's easiest to frame the niche if its width is between two studs (about 15 inches). If you wish to make a wider niche, you can cut out part of a stud, but you'll need to replace it with trimmer studs if it's a load-bearing wall (see diagram).

You can cut a niche opening in existing drywall with a reciprocating saw, or just plan it on an open stud wall. If you're cutting through drywall, you need to be careful about cutting through wires or pipes that may be behind the wall. If you're planning a wider niche, cut out that part of the stud you'll need to frame it. Install a horizontal 2x4 nailer at the top of where you want the niche to be; if you need to take a stud out of a load-bearing wall, install a double 2x6 or larger header instead. Install trimmer studs if you need them, and the sill, which can just be a 2x4 support or a piece of shelving with a dadoed end (or a piece of molding). If you're installing a preformed niche with an arched top, you'll need to install diagonal supports at the top to provide a nailing base for the top of the niche. Finish drywalling the rest of the wall.

STRAIGHTENING A STUD

Studs that are only slightly misaligned ($\frac{1}{4}$ inch or so) because of a framing error can often be repositioned with a whack from a heavy framing hammer. Toenailing a couple of nails can sometimes pull a straight piece into place. If studs are straight and measure less than $\frac{1}{4}$ inch out of alignment, leave them alone. However, defective studs may have to be straightened or even replaced if they bulge out into the plane on which you intend to fasten drywall.

Tools and Materials

Difficulty Level:

- 4-foot level
- Handsaw or circular saw
- 2-foot-long scab boards to match your framing
- 8-foot 2×6
- 12- to 24-inch pipe or bar clamp
- Hammer or screw gun
- 10d nails or 2½-inch screws

1. CUT KERFS.

Using a handsaw or a circular saw (being careful to avoid kickback), cut a 1-inch-deep kerf into the concave edge of each stud that is bowing outward.

2. ATTACH A BOARD AND CLAMP IT.

Fasten a 2×6 board across several studs on the side you have kerfed. Then attach a clamp between the other side of the curved stud and the board, as shown in the illustration.

3. STRAIGHTEN AND STABILIZE THE STUD.

Tighten the clamp: the kerf will open up, and the concave side of the stud will come even with the 2×6. Nail or screw on a scab board to the side of the stud to keep it straight. Then remove the clamp and the 2×6.

1. *To straighten a bowed stud, cut a kerf with a handsaw or circular saw at the center of the bow on the concave edge.*

2. *Attach a 2x6 across several studs on the side you have kerfed, and then fasten a clamp around the stud and the 2x6.*

3. *Tighten the clamp until the stud is flush with the board. Then attach a scab to the stud, and remove the clamp and board.*

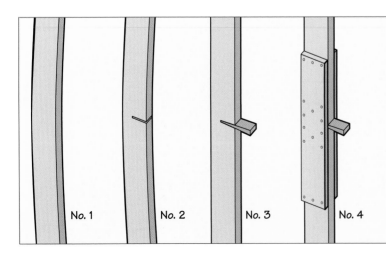

No. 1   No. 2   No. 3   No. 4

An alternative method is shown at left. Kerf the concave side of the stud with a handsaw or circular saw (illustration number 2). Then take a wooden wedge of some sufficiently hard wood, and drive it into the kerf with a hammer as you pull the stud toward you to open up the kerf (illustration number 3). The wedge will force apart the kerf much as the clamp does in the sequence above. Check the stud with a 4-ft. level for straightness between hammer blows. When the stud is straight, attach scab boards to stabilize it (illustration number 4). You can leave the wedge in place by using a handsaw to cut it off flush or remove it for use elsewhere.

Soundproofing

Gypsum wallboard alone has sound-deadening properties, but in some situations you may want to add extra protection from noise—for example, in the wall between a shop and living areas or between a bedroom and kitchen. Sound passes between rooms through any small opening, and walls, floors, and ceilings transmit vibrations. Your first step is to seal up any openings that might be letting sound leak through. Once you've taken care of those, you can use a number of different techniques to deaden vibrations.

➤ *If your shop or garage is unfinished, fill the bays between studs with batts of fiberglass insulation, and cover the unfinished side with ¹/₂-in. or thicker wallboard. This alone will eliminate a great deal of noise on the other side of the wall.*

➤ *Even better, install a second layer on the shop side—preferably on top of steel hat channel. These metal tracks raise a panel off the surface below, keeping the topmost panel from transmitting the sound efficiently to the surface beneath it. Install the channels horizontally 6 in. below the ceiling and 2 in. above the floor, no more than 2 ft. apart.*

➤ *Instead of installing a second layer of drywall, try adding acoustical tiles to the noisy side of the partition. Simply spread adhesive on the back of the panels and screw them down, using fasteners long enough to penetrate into the framing beneath. This material will provide even more noise reduction than drywall.*

➤ *If you're building a new structure and can plan ahead for it, staggered-stud framing offers excellent sound-deadening qualities. For this technique, use a 2x6 plate, and align adjacent 2x4 studs with opposite edges of the plate, 12 in. on center. Weave fiberglass insulation into the gap between the studs. The two faces of the wall have no direct contact with each other, except at the top and bottom plates, which reduces noise transmission even more.*

➤ *A layer of acoustical tile or specially made sound-deadening board, when sandwiched between layers of ¹/₂-in.-thick drywall, is just as effective at deadening sound transmission as a staggered-stud wall; it will make even the loudest machinery (or people) barely audible on the other side.*

Wall Description

Sound Transmission Class & Comfort Level

Typical utility area stud wall 16" O.C., unfinished on one side.

½" Drywall

STC 28

½" Drywall on both sides of 16" O.C. stud wall.

STC 39

16" O.C. Insulated Stud Wall

Extra Layer Drywall

Steel Channel

STC 44

Sound Source

16" O.C. Insulated Stud Wall

Inner Layer of ½" Drywall

Acoustical Tile

STC 46

2x4 Studs Staggered 12" O.C.

Blanket Insulation

STC 50

16" O.C. Insulated Stud Wall

Outer Layer of ½" Drywall

Middle Layer of ½" Sound-Deadening Board

Inner Layer of ½" Drywall

STC 50

Furring Walls and Ceilings. *Small in size but large in importance, shims help correct minor errors in many aspects of framing. They can be used to realign window and door frames or to even out furring strips on an uneven surface.*

Furring Walls & Ceilings

Drywall panels are not always fastened directly to studs, joists, or old walls. Occasionally, the situation calls for furring strips, which are especially useful when the framing or surface you intend to cover is out of level or plumb. Milled from softwood (spruce, pine, or fir) and sold in bundles, furring strips measure 1½ inches wide and ⅝ to 1 inch thick (depending on the desired standoff). Steel furring strips are also available. *Furring* refers to the entire process of attaching the strips and shimming them to a consistent plane.

When drywall is attached to standard-thickness furring, it stands ⅝ inch off the wall, which is ideal if the wall has an inconsistent plaster or masonry surface. Because furring is attached directly to the studs, joists, or existing surface, it may need to be shimmed at low spots in an old wall. If you come across a

noticeable high spot, try to bring the bulge down if you can. Otherwise, you'll have to measure how far the bump protrudes and fur out at least that far, planing the strips or skipping over that spot to adjust for the bulge. When adjusting for low spots, use a straightedge, level, or string-and-block standoff method to determine where you'll need to use shims.

The Pros Know

Furring is a great time-saving way of finishing your basement perimeter walls, but if you have a basement with moisture problems, you might want to think twice about it. A row of nail-holes can easily turn into a crack, which can easily lead to leaks—and water-soaked drywall, among other problems. To avoid this, use 2x2s or 2x4s not as furring but to frame an entirely new wall. You don't have to nail them in, and it leaves more room for insulation, too.

FURRING OVER MASONRY OR PLASTER

Tools and Materials

Difficulty Level: 🐦🐦

- Basic hand tools
- Mastic adhesive
- Caulking gun
- Chalk-line box
- Drill & screw gun
- Fasteners
- Masonry bit, if anchors are used
- Furring
- 4-foot level
- Plumb bob
- String & blocks

1. MAKE YOUR LAYOUT.

After dampproofing, if necessary, clean the wall you intend to fur out, removing any loose masonry or plaster. Decide whether to install drywall horizontally or vertically, and then lay out your furring strips accordingly. Long strips provide a nail or screw base along the long panel edges, whereas shorter strips provide backing for end-butt joints or for the edges of vertical panels.

2. SNAP CHALK LINES.

Snap a vertical chalk line every 16 or 24 inches on center on a masonry wall. Use a level or plumb bob to make sure the chalk lines are plumb. For a plaster wall, locate the studs beneath the plaster using an electronic stud finder, and snap chalk lines on stud locations.

3. CHECK THE WALL FOR IRREGULARITIES.

Run a level or straightedge perpendicular to these chalk lines and locate any low spots or bulges. Mark them with chalk or a pencil. (See "Shimming Furring" on page 55.)

2. To properly position furring on a masonry wall, snap chalk lines at the proper on-center spacing (based on your 16- or 24-in.-on-center layout marks) to guide furring placement. (When furring over an old plaster wall, match the on-center spacing of the studs beneath.)

1. Furring is an ideal nailing base to install over masonry surfaces. It can be easily shimmed to present a plumb plane on which to attach drywall panels.

3. To determine whether shimming is required behind furring strips, place a straightedge on the wall to see whether there is a gap behind it. If so, the wall is recessed at this point, and shimming may be required.

4. PREPARE THE FURRING STRIPS.

Predrill the furring strips every 16 inches for the fasteners. Hold the strips up to your chalk lines, and mark the wall where the fasteners will be located by poking through the holes with a pencil. Set the strips aside, and drill the wall for your fasteners. (You can skip these steps if you're using PAFs, masonry nails, or hardened-steel cut nails.) If your fastening system requires them, install anchor shields.

5. ATTACH THE FURRING STRIPS.

Apply adhesive to the back of a strip, and using the chalk lines as a guide, place it in position. Next, use fasteners to firmly attach the two ends of the strip to the masonry. Repeat for each strip. If possible, hold off on tightening the fasteners down until you've completed the shimming.

6. CHECK FURRING WITH STRING-AND-BLOCK METHOD.

Using a straightedge, level, or string-and-block standoff method, check to see that your furring strips form a flat surface. Take care of any bulges, and then insert shims as described in "Shimming Furring" on page 55. Complete the process of attaching all the fasteners.

5. After inserting shields or anchors (if used), apply construction adhesive to the backs of the furring strips, and then attach the ends of each strip.

4. Hold the predrilled furring strip in position, make sure it's plumb, and use the holes to mark where to drill for bolt anchors.

6. Finish attaching the furring strips to the wall (shimming where needed), using screws, nails, or PAFs. (See "Choosing the Right Masonry Fastener," opposite.)

CHOOSING THE RIGHT MASONRY FASTENER

When attaching wood to masonry, you'll need special fasteners. You can choose from three basic types: hammered, powder-actuated, or shield-and-anchor.

Hammered fasteners are designed to be driven through furring and into masonry with a heavy hammer. These include spiral masonry nails and cut nails, which are heavy, flat, and tapered. Unfortunately, nails present a serious drawback: you don't have room for error when driving them. A glancing blow can loosen the nail. On the plus side, you don't have to predrill your masonry and furring strips, a requirement of shield-and-anchor systems.

Powder-actuated fasteners (PAFs) are pins that you shoot through the furring and into the masonry. This takes a special handheld tool that discharges a .22 caliber cartridge for each pin it drives. (*Use extreme caution: if a PAF is misused, the pin can act like a bullet.*) PAFs work only with concrete, not bricks or cinder blocks. The charges come in several different sizes that are color-coded to match the strength of the concrete.

Make sure you select a charge that neither overdrives the nail (through the furring strip) nor leaves the nailhead exposed. The nailhead should lie flush with or just below the furring's surface. (Experiment with different charges until you find the right one.) PAFs offer a twofold advantage: you can work very quickly, and you don't have to predrill the masonry and furring strips as you do when using a shield-and-anchor system.

Shield-and-anchor systems consist of two parts. You insert the tapered lead or plastic shields (expanding tubes) into predrilled holes in the masonry. When you drive the screws (matched to the shields) through the furring, they expand the shields, gripping the sides of the hole and resisting withdrawal.

FURRING OVER STUD AND JOIST FRAMING

Attaching furring strips directly to framing ensures that the nailing surface for drywall is as level (for ceilings) or plumb (for walls) as possible. A remodeling job will usually expose old and sometimes irregular framing. Newly framed structures or rooms may not require furring (depending on the quality of the lumber and the skill of the framing crew). In either situation, you may want to install furring strips if you suspect that studs or joists are out of true. Properly installed, furring can provide a plumb or level nailing surface.

Fluted-shank
Masonry Nail

Hardened-steel
Cut Nail

Masonry nails and certain cut nails are designed to be driven through lumber into masonry.

PAFs, which are shot through wood and into masonry using a .22 caliber cartridge, are a reliable way to fasten wood to concrete. Caution: follow manufacturer's instructions carefully.

Specialty bolts or pins can be screwed into expanding anchors. The anchors must be set in place in predrilled holes, and this requires some careful planning when spacing your furring.

When attaching furring strips to existing framing, install them perpendicular to the framing members. In walls, this means the furring will be horizontal, which will require horizontal placement of drywall panels. In ceilings, the strips will run across (rather than along) the joists. This will have little bearing on the orientation of the panels, or on which way the joints run.

Between the ends of the furring strips (for instance, along the top and bottom of the wall), you'll need to install filler furring to provide a nail base for panel edges along the ends of the wall. This will ensure that all drywall edges and ends will be solidly backed.

Tools and Materials

Difficulty Level: 🐢🐢

- Basic hand tools
- Chalk-line box
- Furring
- 4-foot level
- Plumb bob
- Screw gun or drill
- String and blocks
- 2½-inch common nails or drywall screws

1. LAY OUT YOUR LINES ON THE STUDS.

Determine the spacing for your furring, either 16 or 24 inches on center. (If you have a choice, go with 16 inches, which will make the drywall more rigid.) On walls, snap chalk lines at the proper intervals, using a level and measuring tape to position them accurately. On ceilings, lay out the spacing with a measuring tape, and then snap chalk lines across the undersides of the joists.

2. CHECK THE WALL FOR STRAIGHTNESS.

For walls, use a level (or any long straightedge) to check for irregularities in the framing members. Mark the recesses or bulges on the edge of the studs. Use the same procedure for checking the ceiling framing.

3. INSTALL THE HORIZONTAL FURRING STRIPS.

Attach the horizontal furring strips, but screw or nail just the ends so that the strips can be easily shimmed. Using the string-and-block standoff method and noting your pencil marks from the previous step, shim the furring or shave the framing (high spots) as necessary to achieve a flat plane.

The Pros Know

When drywalling over furring strips, any electrical outlet or switch boxes that have already been installed will look sunken into the drywall. But electrical boxes can be fitted with a box extender: just turn off the power, remove the faceplate, and unscrew the fixture from the box. Slide the extender over the fixture and wiring and onto the box. Use the longer bolts that come with the extender to reattach the fixture to the box, making sure to adjust the extender's position so that the fixture will be flush with the new wall.

1. *Mark the position of furring strips on the studs by snapping chalk lines based on your layout marks.*

2. *Use a straightedge to check the wall for irregularities. Any recesses may have to be shimmed beneath the furring.*

3. *Install the horizontal furring strips, but screw down just the ends so they can be easily shimmed.*

Shimming Furring

Whether you're drywalling over masonry, framing, or old plaster, it's imperative that you create a surface that is both flat and plumb (for walls) or level (for ceilings). By inserting shims (cedar shingles) behind furring strips before fastening them down, you can compensate for any low spots in a wall. This simple process involves three steps: detecting low spots, shimming them one by one, and then screwing or nailing the strips permanently in place.

Once you've snapped chalk lines to lay out your furring, survey the wall for obvious low spots by holding a straightedge (a 4-foot level) against the wall. Orient it in the same direction that your furring strips will run. Mark any low spots along the length of your chalk lines.

Install the furring strips, but fasten them only at the ends. Using the string-and-block standoff method, determine which strips protrude or recede. At the receding (low) spots, insert shims behind the strips. For large gaps, use opposing shims. (See the drawing at right.)

Finally, drive nails or screws through the furring strips and shims into the wall. Wherever possible, anchor the furring to the existing framing beneath.

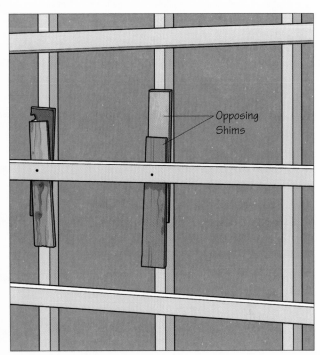

Shimming Furring. Use a level or string and blocks to check your furring for low spots, and shim those areas up to the correct plane of the rest of the wall.

3 Wall & Ceiling Prep

4. INSTALL THE VERTICAL STRIPS AND SHIMS.

Install shorter strips where the ends of the drywall will fall. Leave a ¼-inch gap at each end where the vertical strips meet the horizontal ones. (Use 14-inch short strips between 16-inch on-center horizontal furring, or 22-inch short strips between 24-inch on-center furring.) Shim the furring as necessary, and then finish nailing or screwing the strips into place.

4. *Attach the filler furring strips between the main courses of furring, and then install the remaining fasteners.*

INSTALLING METAL FURRING ON A CEILING

You have several options when it comes to installing a ceiling in the basement. You can hang a suspended ceiling, which uses a grid to hold acoustical tiles. This option might be better if you must have access to utilities like electrical or plumbing and you can afford to lose a few inches of headroom. According to most building codes, each room in a finished basement must have a minimum of 90 inches of headroom (84 inches in kitchens, hallways, and bathrooms) over at least half of its area.

If headroom is tight, you should install drywall and paint it or glue acoustical tile to it. Don't attach drywall directly to the underside of the ceiling joists, however; use resilient steel furring channels attached perpendicular to the joists and shimmed where needed.

Tools and Materials

Difficulty Level: 🔶🔶

- ◾ String & shims
- ◾ Screw gun
- ◾ Chalk-line box
- ◾ Resilient metal channels
- ◾ Aviation snips
- ◾ Sheet-metal screws

1. CHECK AND MARK THE JOISTS.

In some basements the ceiling joists may be incon-sistent—this can cause an unevenness in the finished surface. Before you install the ceiling channel tracks, use the string-and-block method to check for level, and note any high spots, which you'll have to shave, or low spots, which you'll have to shim. Then snap chalk lines across the joists at 16 or 24 inches on-center to act as guidelines for installing the metal furring.

2. CUT THE FURRING.

If you need to cut the furring to fit the width of the ceiling, use aviation snips to cut the two flanges; then bend back the track and cut the web.

3. INSTALL THE FURRING.

Set a ceiling channel track in place along your chalk lines, and attach it by driving 1½-inch drywall nails or screws into the flanges on each side at each joist. As you install the channel, use a level to double-check for consistency from row to row. Shim where necessary.

When you've leveled, shimmed, and installed the fur-ring, apply drywall as you would to any ceiling, using the Type S screw schedule on page 82.

2. *You may need to cut the furring strips to fit. Use aviation or metal snips to cut the flanges of the metal strip; then bend it back and cut across the webbing.*

1. *Lay out for the ceiling channels, in this case 16 in. on center, and then snap chalk lines.*

3. *Screw the ceiling channels into place along the guidelines. Use a 4-ft. level to ensure that the channels are in a level plane.*

Steel Framing Systems

STEEL-FRAMED WALLS

Steel has long been the material of choice for commercial buildings, but not for houses. However, while lumber prices increase and lumber quality decreases, both the cost and strength of steel has stayed steady.

Steel doesn't warp, shrink, or split like wood, and it isn't food for insects. It won't rot from water leaks—though it may corrode over long exposure. Steel doesn't make a house fireproof, but it won't contribute fuel to a fire, and it keeps the structure intact long after a burning wood frame would collapse. That's one reason why metal framing is standard in commercial construction. Unlike lumber, which can be—and these days increasingly is—riddled with defects, steel studs are never warped, checked, or green.

Even well-built modern homes with wood frames are likely to undergo some shifting and settling that can pop drywall nails and trim joints—or worse. These problems are greatly reduced with steel. It doesn't hold water, so metal studs won't shrink and twist the way wood often does, particularly in the first year after construction when wet wood dries out during the heating season. Also, steel framing members are lighter than solid wood, and put less load on the foundation, which can reduce cracking and faults in masonry as well.

Residential steel construction initially caught on along the West Coast, where the extra strength was valuable against earthquakes, and then in the Southeast to resist damage from hurricanes. It continues, gradually, to gain favor with contractors and homebuyers. Fewer than 15,000 houses were built with steel framing in 1993, but 11 years later it was closer to 200,000.

Typical steel construction involves 20-gauge metal studs about the shape of 2×4s, but with one open side (like a letter C in cross section). These studs are attached (generally with sheet-metal screws) to U-shaped tracks attached to the floor and ceiling. In situations with concrete floors, the bottom track is easily secured with powder-actuated fasteners (PAFs).

Steel Framing Systems. *Steel framing has its advantages, among them the ability to easily execute custom effects such as this multilevel ceiling.*

Steel studs are generally spaced 16 to 24 inches on center, the same as wood framing. These light-gauge studs are only used for non-load-bearing interior walls; they're not strong enough to support loads (without being sistered together). But a do-it-yourselfer without experience in steel construction can

The Pros Know

You might be asking, "I'm not building a skyscraper—why do I need to know about steel framing?" Building a partition wall in a finished house is a perfect example of when steel framing is a good idea: you already have a ceiling and floor framing to attach the tracks to, and you don't have to worry about bearing loads. Steel studs are not only cheaper than wood, but they're easier to handle—one person can carry a bundle of ten—and fire resistant.

easily use steel systems to construct partition walls—and at a lower cost than lumber. Large drywall-supply houses will usually carry steel-framing supplies.

PREPARING STEEL FRAMING FOR DRYWALL

There is only minimal preparation before attaching drywall to steel-framed walls. You should check the framing for straightness as you would with wood (although it's most likely going to be straight). You'll also have to check the orientation of the studs themselves. The open side of the C-shaped channels should all be facing in the same direction.

You'll install the panels of a wall starting in the corner that the open end of the stud faces. If you install the panels in the opposite direction, to the solid side first and then the open side, the screw might bend the open end outward, causing the panels to abut unevenly. Use bugle-head screws with self-tapping points to install the drywall—ordinary drywall screws are capable of drilling through 20-gauge steel, but in the process they will dig out a hole in the drywall larger than the head of the screw, creating finishing problems and unstable drywall.

The panels should ideally all be cut so that the edges break exactly halfway across the stud. If you need to add blocking, clip away the ¼-inch lip that forms the mouth of the "C," and screw a piece of plywood on the inside of the studs. For more detail on installing drywall on steel studs, see "Installing Drywall on a Steel-Framed Wall," pages 93–94.

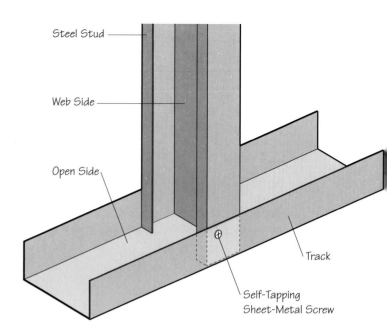

Steel studs have one open side with ¼-in. lips; the web side of studs have holes precut to allow for wires.

In standard steel framing, headers, plates, and sills are cut from the track, which takes the place of the top and bottom plates.

Suspended Ceilings

If you want to install a perfectly flat ceiling over old drywall with a hilly topography—or even over brand-new framing that seems out of whack—using a steel-frame suspended ceiling system might turn out to be easier than endlessly fussing with furring and shims. Modern suspension systems (such as USG's Drywall Suspension System) are substantially easier to install than the old cold-rolled or hat channel systems: tees snap together, eliminating laborious fastening with ties and checking for square, and both the channels and the hanger wire are easier to cut.

The Pros Know

Hanging 100-percent level channels for a suspended ceiling system can be a headache with a water level, and a full-blown migraine with just a measuring tape and a spirit level. If you can spare the expense, a truly liberating tool to add to the collection is a hand-held laser level—it will cast a perfectly level beam of light all the way around the room, eliminating doubts and a whole lot of painstaking measuring and rechecking.

INSTALLING A SUSPENDED CEILING SYSTEM

Tools and Materials

Difficulty Level:

- Basic hand tools
- Measuring tape
- Water level
- 4-foot level
- Resilient metal channels
- Hanger ties
- Screws (sheet-metal and drywall Type S)
- Screw gun
- Aviation snips

1. INSTALL THE TRACK.

Using a water level (or, if available, a laser level), mark the desired elevation where you want the *drywall* to go. (Keep in mind that the drywall will be ¹/₂ to ⁵/₈ inch below the suspension system—depending on drywall thickness—and that most building codes require at least 90 inches of headroom in normal living spaces. Check with your local building inspector before planning a suspended ceiling.) Now mark the line where you will install the track, which will support the ceiling framing. Install the track—either channel molding (which is C-shaped) or wall angle (which is L-shaped)—into the studs at the top of the wall using sheet-metal screws. Periodically check the track for level as you install it.

2. INSTALL THE MAIN TEES.

Main tees generally come in 10- or 12-foot lengths. If one of your room's dimensions happens to be 10 or 12 feet, make this the dimension across which you will place the main tees. Otherwise, you will have to cut the main tees to fit a shorter dimension or splice two of them together (using hanger wire or specially-made splicing clips available where you purchase the tees) to fit a longer dimension. Place the main tees on the track every 2 feet. Check the tees for level, and then attach the hanger wires from the main tees to the existing ceiling joists, to provide additional support for the ceiling.

3. INSTALL THE CROSS TEES.

Install the cross tees perpendicular to the main tees every 16 or 24 inches on center. (Cross tees are manufactured in 2-foot lengths to fit in between the main tees.) This will provide a level surface and sufficient support for drywalling. Follow the ceiling installation procedures for drywall as outlined in Chapter 5, pages 83–84. Use Type S screws and the ceiling screw schedule on page 82.

1. *After you've marked the elevation with a level, you're ready to install the track around the perimeter of the room. Screw it into the studs using metal screws.*

2. *Main tees will be installed 24 in. on center. Cut or splice them as needed to the proper length, and snap them into the track. Attach hanger wires for additional support.*

3. *Cross tees are installed under the main tees every 16 or 24 in. on center. They come in 24-in. lengths to fit between the main tees.*

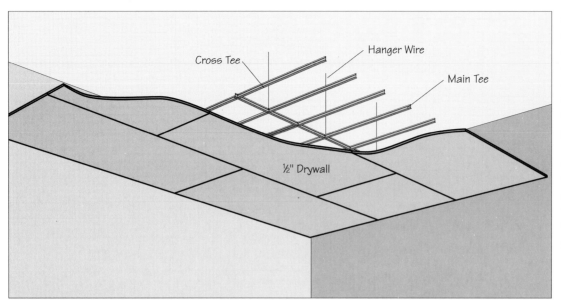

Cross Tee

Hanger Wire

Main Tee

½" Drywall

Metal suspended ceiling systems require no special equipment to install. Lightweight steel is screwed into a track and tied to existing joists with hanger wire. Suspension systems are usually compatible with acoustical tiles and lighting panels, if you wish to mix these with drywall in your installation.

SUSPENDED DRYWALL FASCIA AND SCULPTURED CEILINGS

Advances in both suspension systems and flexible drywall have permitted designers to be much more adventurous in their use of curves—not just in walls, but in multilevel ceilings and serpentine soffit boxes. It's something that is most effective when used minimally, but a room can be given a great deal of flair at minimal expense—without having a frame of fancy curves in wood—with the addition of an undulating corner or recessed ceiling panel. Think of them as partial dropped ceilings. Special curved main tees and trim are available, so any shape can be dropped down from the main joists: circles, serpentine boxes, any kind of shape you can imagine.

Suspended ceiling systems (right) make it easy to add a sculptural effect to your ceiling with elegant soffits.

Wall Channel

Cross Tee

¼" Flexible Drywall

Curved Main Tee

Curved soffits are easy to create with metal suspension systems. Just use the curved main tees (visible at left) spaced 48 in. on center, and space the regular cross tees tighter (9 in. on center). Curved cross tees are also available for making S-shape boxes. Just follow the recommendation for installing drywall on curved walls (pages 94–96).

3 Wall & Ceiling Prep

Splayed Hanger Wire

Main Tee Splice Plate

Curved Main Tee

12 Ga. Hanger Wire

Main Tee

Flexible Drywall Panels

Cross Tees

Knurled Channel Molding

Vaults provide a distinctive design touch and are a good way to customize any drywall application. Place hanger wires a maximum of 48 in. along the main tee. For stability, drywall joints should be a minimum of 12 in. from main tee splices.

Vaults and valleys can be created using metal suspension systems such as the one shown here. Splayed hanger wires add stability to the curved sections of drywall. For curved sections, use flexible drywall panels recommended by the manufacturer.

Splayed Hanger Wires

12 Ga. Hanger Wire

Splice Clip

Curved Main Tee

Main Tee

Cross Tees

Flexible Drywall Panels

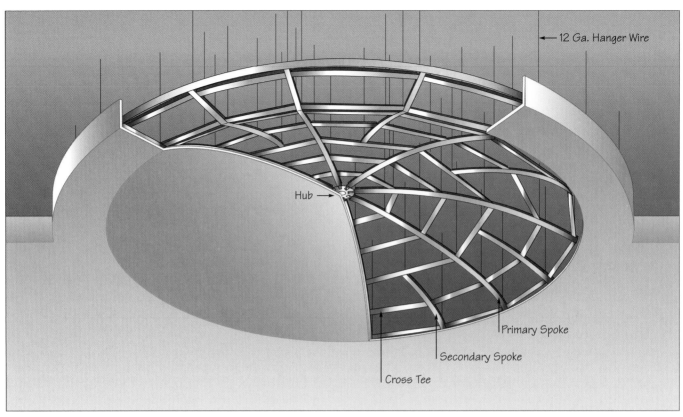

12 Ga. Hanger Wire

Hub

Primary Spoke

Secondary Spoke

Cross Tee

Boxed soffits are easier than ever before to create with metal suspension systems. In fact, this system uses the same components used on flat surface areas. The maximum vertical soffit height is 48 in. with cross tees spaced 24 in. on center.

Dome suspension systems do away with bending steel on the job site. The system shown here features a prefabricated hub and preformed curved tees for easy installation. Hanger wires should be placed a maximum of 32 in. along each spoke.

Cross Tee

12 Ga. Hanger Wire

Cross Tee

Drywall Panel

Chapter 4

Marking & Cutting

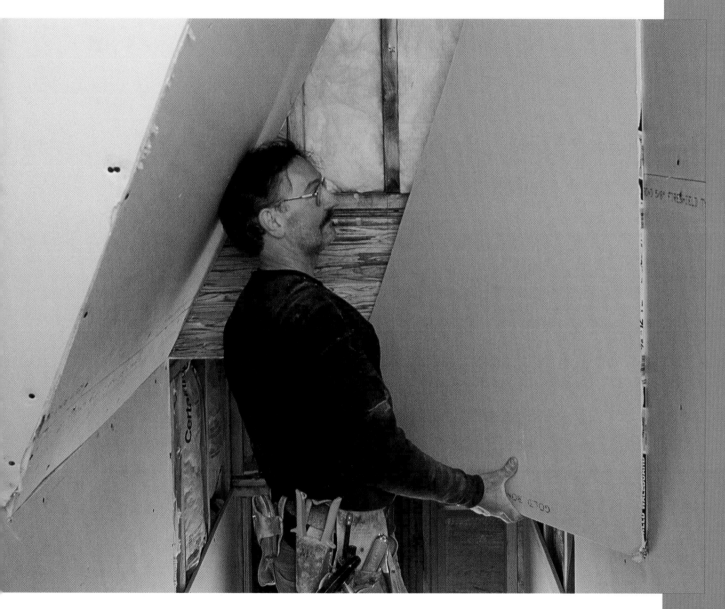

Precise measuring and marking of angles and cutouts can make the critical difference between a professional-looking job and a second-rate attempt at drywalling. You can ruin the appearance of hours' worth of precise square cuts on a long wall section with a single inaccurately cut archway or a misplaced cutout for a utility box.

*T*here's no deep secret to measuring and marking drywall, but a few tricks of the trade and specialty tools will streamline your efforts and improve your accuracy. Once you've got the hang of marking holes and angles, you can test the various tools and techniques to aid you in making precise (and, where possible, dustless) cuts in drywall panels.

Straight Cut Lines

Marking straight cut lines on drywall requires a keen eye and the right tools. A straight cut line usually refers to one that is square to an edge or end of the panel. Because the manufacturer's edge serves as a dependable reference, most methods for squaring lines on drywall rely on the edge as a guide. The following procedure calls for a T-square, but you can also use a smaller tool, such as a combination or framing square.

MARKING CUT LINES USING A T-SQUARE

Tools and Materials

Difficulty Level:

- Drywall panels
- Measuring tape or folding rule
- Pencil
- Utility knife
- 4-foot T-square

1. MEASURE YOUR CUT LINES.
Use a measuring tape to determine the size of the piece you need, and then locate these dimensions on the drywall panel.

2. MARK THE LINES ON THE PANEL.
Place the 4-foot T-square against the panel so that the long blade is parallel with the cut line you intend to make. Slide the T-square along the edge or end of the panel until the edge of its blade lines up with the mark you made. Run your pencil along the blade, marking your cut line. Repeat this step for the per-

Straight Cut Lines. For short, straight cuts in a piece of drywall, a sharp drywall or utility saw and a steady cutting motion are all that is needed.

pendicular cut line, if one is needed. Before making any cut, make sure your utility knife has a sharp blade, and wear eye protection. Using a straightedge as your guide, score the face (good) side of the dry-wall to a depth of 1/8 inch.

3. SNAP THE CUT BACK.
Working from the cut side (*or* the side opposite the cut), use a quick motion to snap the panel along the cut line, and fold it back slightly. Don't try to tear the cut panel; just let the panel break along your cut line. The panel should now be held together just by the paper backing.

4. SCORE THE BACK, AND SEPARATE THE PIECES.
Using your utility knife, score the back side of the panel to cut through the paper, and then separate the two pieces.

1. Use the measurements you took from the wall, and transfer them onto the panel you intend to install. One mark at the top of the panel is usually sufficient.

2. Using the T-square, first draw your cut line on the face of the panel. Then, using your foot to seat the bottom of the square, make the cut using a utility knife.

3. Using one motion, snap the panel back along the cut line. (Work in front of or behind the panel.)

4. Using a utility knife, cut through the paper on the back of the panel, and separate the pieces.

MARKING CUT LINES USING A CHALK LINE

Snapping a chalk line marks a long, straight line quickly and accurately. It works especially well on diagonal lines. The trick is to locate and mark dimensions on the adjacent edge and end of a panel, and then snap a chalk line between them.

Tools and Materials

Difficulty Level: ⬛

- Drywall panels
- Measuring tape or folding rule
- Pencil
- Utility knife
- Chalk-line box

1. MEASURE YOUR CUT LINES.

Using a measuring tape, locate the dimensions of the drywall piece you require onto opposite edges or ends of the drywall panel.

2. SNAP CHALK LINES ON THE PANEL.

Using these reference marks, snap chalk lines across the full length or width (or diagonal) of the panel.

3. CUT THE LINES.

Using a utility knife, score and snap cut lines as described on pages 64–65.

2. If necessary, seat the string in a small notch made with the utility knife on the first mark. Run the chalk line between the two marks you have made on the panel, and snap it, leaving a straight chalk mark.

1. Locate the dimensions of the piece you need onto a panel or piece of a panel.

3. Using your utility knife, cut the line you have made. Snap the panel back along the cut line, and then cut from the back.

USING THE COORDINATE METHOD FOR MARKING AND CUTTING OPENINGS

For most walls, you have to make cutouts for utility boxes (outlets and fixtures), switches, pipes, and services (such as ductwork and supply lines for hydronic baseboards). It's easy to overlook a switch or outlet—you should always double-check before installing a panel. If you neglect to make a cutout, you'll have to take down the drywall because there's no accurate way to locate the box once the panel is up. If just the subflooring has been installed where you're working, you may want to mark the location of each light switch and power outlet on the plywood using a permanent marker. You could do the same using masking tape on finished flooring or carpeting.

To use the coordinate method for marking and cutting holes, you treat the drywall panel as if it were a piece of graph paper. To locate a point or outline a box, draw intersecting lines from an adjacent edge and end of the panel.

Tools and Materials

Difficulty Level: ⬛

- Drywall panels
- Measuring tape or folding rule
- Pencil
- Utility knife
- 4-foot T-square
- Utility saw

1. LOCATE THE REQUIRED HOLE ON THE PANEL.

On the wall where you'll attach the drywall panel, measure to the near sides of the switch or outlet you must accommodate. To get accurate dimensions, start your measurements at the corner and ceiling (or floor) against which the panel will finally sit. Then lay out these dimensions on the panel: for example, 25 inches in from the right and 32 inches down from the top. For a round hole, you'll need to note only the centerpoint of the circle. For a rectangular cutout, measure to the far sides of the box, and then transfer all four sides to the piece of drywall.

2. DRAW THE OUTLINE OF THE HOLE ON THE PANEL.

Using the 4-foot T-square or a measuring tape, connect the coordinate points of the box on the panel face. If you have a utility box handy that is identical to the one in question, measure to the far corner point of the existing box, line up the spare one with the point, and trace a pencil outline around the box.

1. By finding the X and Y (vertical and horizontal) coordinates for a utility box, you can transfer those measurements to a piece of drywall and precisely cut out a rectangle that will allow the box to protrude.

2. Use a T-square to transfer your coordinate measurements to the panel, and draw a box to be cut away. (Or trace the outline of a spare box.)

3. CUT OUT THE HOLE.

Drill a starter hole through one corner of the box or near the circle's perimeter, and then cut along the line with a utility knife or saw. Hold the panel in place to verify that the hole lines up with the box. Trim the hole to enlarge it if necessary.

3. *Cut out the piece. When cutting out for utility boxes, be sure the cutout section is precise; inaccurately cut corners can result in face damage when the drywall is pushed into place.*

USING THE HAMMER-AND-BLOCK METHOD

Because drywall is relatively soft, it shows indentations where objects have hit or pressed against it. Here's a method for marking utility boxes that takes advantage of this characteristic.

Tools and Materials

Difficulty Level: 🔨

- ◼ Hammer
- ◼ 8-inch 2x4 block
- ◼ Utility saw

1. SET THE PANEL IN PLACE.

Before making any utility-box cutouts, place the drywall panel in position against the studs or wall, just as if you were installing it.

2. TAP THE PANEL OVER THE UTILITY BOXES.

Place a piece of scrap wood against the panel wherever a box is located, and tap the wood lightly with a hammer. The edges of the box should make a slight indentation in the panel's back face.

3. CUT OUT THE HOLE.

Remove the drywall panel, jab a utility saw through one of the corners of the indentation, and then cut out the opening. Reinstall the panel, and fasten it in place.

1. *One alternative method of marking for a utility box is to position the drywall where it will be installed, and place a block over the box's location.*

2. *When you gently hammer the block, the utility box will leave an imprint on the back of the drywall panel, indicating the shape to be cut out.*

If you're doing several rooms, you may find it worthwhile to get a utility-box cutout locator. This device attaches to the utility box on the wall. When you press the panel into position, the sticky face of the locator adheres itself to the drywall. You simply trace around the locator and then remove it.

3. *Turn the sheet around and, following the outline, carefully cut out the hole using a utility saw. Be careful not to damage the face.*

The Pros Know

If you have soft chalk or can find a tube of lipstick on the premises, apply either substance to the edges of each utility box, and then press the panel into position. This will leave behind an accurate "roadmap" of all boxes on the back of the panel. If you make a cutout that's a bit too small for the utility box, never force the panel in hope that the box will punch cleanly through the drywall. In most cases, the box will damage a corner of the hole instead, leaving you with a labor-intensive patch job. Always enlarge the hole instead of forcing it.

4 Marking & Cutting

Curved Cut Lines

Arched doorways and areas around fancy window wells often require curved cuts. The simplest way to make these cuts is to install the full panel over them and trim the excess by following a utility saw along the top of the curve. Sometimes this isn't possible, such as when a window has already been installed and there's no room to move a saw. To mark these curves with accuracy, you can use a string or make yourself a cardboard template.

If an archway has a consistent curve, it's part of a perfect circle (an arc). If you can determine that circle's radius (the distance from the centerpoint to the circumference), you can draw any part of it using a pencil and string. You may want to practice it first on cardboard—cut along the arc with a utility knife, and compare the resulting template with the area you intend to drywall. (If it fits, simply use it to mark the actual panel.)

If your archway has a flattened or asymmetrical curve, move on to "Marking a Curve Using a Template," pages 70–71.

Curves and Irregular Lines. *Cutting curves into panels before they're installed can be tricky; it's easier to trim them in place if possible.*

MARKING A SEMICIRCLE WITH STRING

Tools and Materials

Difficulty Level: 🔨🔨

- Drywall panel
- Measuring tape
- Pencil
- Nonstretchable string
- Utility knife
- Masking tape
- Utility saw

1. DETERMINE THE RADIUS OF THE ARCH.

For a half-circle, just measure the width of the door and divide by 2; for less than a half-circle, use the method described on page 97. Tie a pencil to a length of nonstretchable string; then mark the radius along the string using a piece of masking tape.

2. TRANSFER THE ARCH TO THE DRYWALL.

Establish the center of the circle on the panel, and hold the string at the tape mark on that point with your thumb. With the string fully extended, swing the pencil across the panel, drawing a curved line that matches your archway. Score the line repeatedly with a utility knife, or use a utility saw to cut out the piece.

2. *Transfer the arc onto a piece of drywall by tacking (or holding with your thumb) the string at one edge of the drywall and swinging the pencil at the limit of the string to the right and left, drawing a curved line as you go.*

1. *To determine the radius of an arc forming a half-circle, first measure the diameter, and then divide by 2. In our example, the diameter is 3 ft. The 18-in. radius can then be transferred to the string and pencil.*

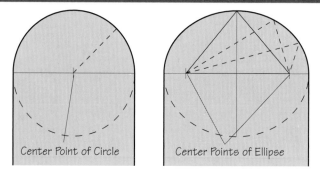

Center Point of Circle   Center Points of Ellipse

Some curves *are not arcs of perfect circles, but of ellipses (which have two center points). The string method used earlier will not work on asymmetrical curves. You must use a template to copy the shape of the archway onto a piece of drywall.*

MARKING A CURVE USING A TEMPLATE

You'll often encounter archways that are asymmetrical—that is, they don't form part of a perfect circle. These curves might be slightly flattened (or flat) at the top, or parts of ellipses or parabolas rather than circles. In these cases, use a cardboard template to transfer the curve onto the drywall.

Tools and Materials

Difficulty Level:

- Drywall panel
- Measuring tape or folding rule
- Pencil
- Cardboard
- Utility knife
- Utility saw

1. MAKE A CARDBOARD TEMPLATE.

Hold a piece of cardboard against the curve, and trace its shape. You can trace a window frame only if the window has not yet been installed. If the window is already in place, cut a rough template, and trim it as needed until it fits the archway exactly. Cut out the template using a utility knife.

2. USE THE TEMPLATE TO MARK THE DRYWALL.

Place the cardboard template on the panel exactly where the curve will occur, and then trace the shape. Use a T-square or chalk-line box to mark any other required cuts.

3. CUT OUT THE ARCHWAY.

Score the cut line repeatedly using a utility knife, or use a utility saw to make the cutout; then install the panel.

2. *Position the curved cardboard template on a piece of drywall where the archway will occur in the final drywall panel installation, and trace the template's shape onto the drywall.*

1. *To create a template, hold a piece of cardboard up to the archway, trace the archway's shape, and cut the cardboard.*

3. *After tracing the archway's shape from the cardboard onto the drywall, use a utility knife or saw to cut out the shape.*

MARKING A ROUND HOLE

Many light fixtures are mounted on (or hang from) square or octagonal utility boxes. For these shapes, use the coordinate method described earlier to draw the cutout. Other fixtures require round holes, as do pipes and some types of ductwork. There are a number of easy ways to cut a circular hole.

Tools and Materials

Difficulty Level: 🔨🔨

- Drywall panel
- Measuring tape or 4-foot T-square
- Pencil
- Compass
- Utility saw

1. MEASURE FOR THE ROUND HOLE.

Use a measuring tape and the coordinate method to determine where the centerpoint of the round hole will fall on the panel you are going to install. (See "Using the Coordinate Method for Marking and Cutting Openings," page 67.) Next, determine the radius of the hole by measuring across the entire width of the fixture or the pipe or duct that you're cutting out for and dividing this measurement by 2.

2. DRAW THE HOLE ON THE DRYWALL.

Set the point of a compass on the centerpoint you've marked and the arm at the radius measurement. Draw the circle onto the drywall.

1. *To cut out a circle in a piece of drywall, first find the coordinates for the center of the circle, and determine the circle's radius. Transfer the centerpoint of the circle to the drywall.*

3. CUT OUT THE HOLE.

Use a utility knife, circle cutter, or utility saw to cut the hole.

2. *Use a compass to mark the circle on the panel. For larger circles, use the string method (p. 70) or a circle cutter (p. 73).*

3. *Cut out the hole using a utility knife or saw. If the hole isn't too small or too large for a circle cutter, you can cut it out more accurately with that tool. (See next page.)*

Special Techniques for Marking & Cutting

SCRIBING DRYWALL TO AN IRREGULAR WALL

Occasionally, drywall abuts or adjoins an irregular wall: a fieldstone hearth, a brick wall, or an out-of-true plaster wall. These situations call for scribing, using a compass or special scriber, which makes it easy to transfer an irregular profile onto a panel.

To do this, position a drywall panel next to the irregular wall or structure exactly as it will sit but an inch or two back from its installed location. Slide the pointed end of the scriber down the irregular profile, keeping it firmly in contact with the masonry or plaster so that the scriber's pencil faithfully reproduces the profile on the face of the panel. Cut along this line using a utility knife or saw.

You can make nearly all cuts in drywall using a sharp utility knife. However, certain specialty tools offer more accuracy and convenience than the knife, particularly for cutting circular holes. There's also a short-cut method for cutting out holes for pipe.

To scribe drywall to an irregular wall, first position the drywall panel square to the wall, and stabilize it so that it doesn't move when you draw on it. Then run a scribe down the face of the irregular wall so that a profile of the wall is drawn on the drywall's face with the scribe's pencil.

The Pros Know

You can create large circles using a non-stretchable string. Locate the center of the circle, and then tie a pencil on the end of a string that is a little longer than the circle's radius. Pin the other end of the string (measured for the radius) at the center of the circle, and keep the string taut as you trace the circle.

USING A CIRCLE CUTTER AND A HOLE SAW

If you're installing a ceiling panel over recessed lighting, which usually calls for several identical, perfectly round holes, you'll want a streamlined technique for cutting them. Instead of pencil and string, use a circle cutter for larger holes—and chuck a hole saw into a drill for small ones. (See next page.)

A circle cutter resembles a beam compass, except that it has a sharp cutting edge instead of a pencil at the end of its adjustable beam. You set the circle cutter's pin at the layout mark on the panel, adjust the beam to the desired radius, and then rotate to cut a perfect circle. (For a quicker job, you can also buy a circle cutter that chucks into a portable drill.)

A circle cutter is an ideal tool for cutting perfect circles in a drywall panel. A pin at the center anchors the tool, and the compass arm has a round blade that scores a perfect circle into drywall. The tool can be adjusted to cut circles of different diameters.

For a series of small holes (and, unfortunately, big clouds of dust), you can load your drill with a special bit called a hole saw. These cylindrical bits have serrated teeth on one end and a shaft that fits your drill chuck on the other. Hole saws cannot be adjusted for size, so you buy them in sets that cover a range of diameters.

MAKING A CUTOUT WITH A ROUTER

Just as routers can be used to cut holes in wood, so they can be used (with a large Forstner or spur bit) to make cutouts in drywall. Use the coordinate or hammer-and-block method to mark a hole location for a pipe or ductwork, and then apply the router (really a special drywall power cutting tool) to the task. It kicks up more dust than manual cutting, but it's fast and accurate.

A hole saw can be attached to any electric drill to cut perfect small holes.

The Pros Know

On a T-square, both the blade and the fence have rule marks stenciled on them that start with zero at the inside corner of the square. As you get accustomed to working with a T-square, you can simply cut along the blade edge with your utility knife, stopping when you get to the needed measurement (anywhere from an inch to 4 feet), and skip the step of pencil-marking the cut line.

A router can make cutouts for utility boxes when fitted with a bit designed for drywall. This is best done with the drywall in place.

CUTTING A PIPE HOLE WITH PIPE

When installing cement-based board in a bathroom, you'll have to cut holes through which the pipes can protrude. When cutting out for these pipes, you can use a leftover piece of the pipe itself as a tool.

Tools and Materials

Difficulty Level:

- ◼ Hammer
- ◼ 12-inch section of pipe
- ◼ Pencil
- ◼ Measuring tape or folding rule
- ◼ Drill with ⅛-inch masonry bit
- ◼ 4-foot T-square

1. MARK THE HOLE ON THE DRYWALL.

Use the coordinate method to locate and mark the center of where the pipe hole will go. (See "Using the Coordinate Method for Marking and Cutting Openings," page 67.) Draw a circle of the same diameter as your pipe centered on this mark. Use the discarded piece of the pipe as your template. (You can also use a compass.)

2. PERFORATE THE HOLE.

Using an 8d nail or a power drill with a ⅛- to ¼-inch masonry bit, perforate the circumference of this circle, driving the nail or drilling through the panel. Make at least 16 or 20 holes around the circumference of the circle—not so many that the holes are touching, but enough the make the circle easy to break.

1. *To mark for small pipes, use a T-square and the coordinate method for locating the center of the pipe's precise location on the wall, which you can then transfer to the drywall panel. With the center of the pipe's location marked on a drywall panel, draw a circle around this mark a scant greater than the diameter of the pipe. Use a section of the pipe as a marking guide.*

2. *To cut out a hole in cement-based tile backer board, locate and mark the pipe's position. Then use a drill with a ⅛-in. masonry bit to drill holes in the drywall around the pipe's outline.*

3. PUNCH OUT THE HOLE USING THE PIPE.
Place the panel on firm backing; then drive a piece of pipe (optimally with sharp edges) through the drywall panel using a hammer.

3. *Once you have poked the small holes in the backer-board panel, take your section of discarded pipe and drive it through the panel. The resulting hole should be a perfect fit for the pipe in question, making the panel easier to finish.*

Recycling Drywall

Once you've finished your drywalling job, you may wonder whether anything beneficial might be done with the considerable heap of scrap gypsum board that you've generated. For that matter, you may not have the option of ignoring the problem. Some municipalities have started banning gypsum drywall from their landfills because it releases hydrogen sulfide gas as it breaks down.

There are companies that will collect scrap drywall for recycling, but most require that it be free of nails, screws, lead paint, and asbestos. In fact, most wallboard these days contains at least some post-consumer recycled gypsum, and the paper backing often is made with a high percentage of recycled paper. Drywall manufacturers have thus moved in a laudable direction, because gypsum usually must be strip-mined at some cost to the environment.

Some drywall is now being buried in cornfields rather than landfills. Farmers have long added pure gypsum (calcium sulfate) to the soil to improve fertility and keep the pH stable. Agricultural researchers have substituted pulverized wallboard—paper and all—and found that it contributes the same benefits as pure gypsum or limestone without adding any heavy metals or other unwanted by-products. Farms in Colorado and California are already using recycled gypsum board for grape, pea, and peanut crops.

Access Panels

When putting up wallboard adjacent to a bathroom, kitchen, or utility room, you may want to create a removable panel that allows access to pipes behind the wall. This way, if the pipes ever require service, you won't have to cut away finished drywall to get to them. Ideally, access panels should be located in an inconspicuous place, such as inside a closet or behind a washing machine.

Access panels resemble any other piece of patched-in drywall, except that you don't tape or finish them in place. To allow removal, set the panel into the wall with four screws, one in each corner, and cover the seams with trim or molding to hide the screwheads. When designing for an access panel, keep in mind that all of the panel's edges must be backed by studs or plates. You may need to install 2×4 or 2×6 blocking to provide support.

CREATING AN ACCESS PANEL

Tools and Materials

Difficulty Level: 🦇🦇

- Basic hand tools
- Utility knife
- Section of drywall panel
- Molding or other trim material
- 2x4 or 2x6 blocking material
- Drywall or trim screws and 8d nails

1. MEASURE YOUR ACCESS PANEL.
Determine the desired dimensions of your access panel. One stud bay width by 3 feet high allows ample space for servicing pipes.

2. PROVIDE SUFFICIENT BACKING FOR THE HOLE.
Install blocking between the studs to support the panel. The centerline of the top and bottom blocking should align with the panel's top and bottom ends, respectively.

3. INSTALL THE ACCESS PANEL, AND FINISH IT WITH MOLDING.
Install drywall as you would on any wall, but allow for the desired dimensions of the access panel. Cut the panel piece from scrap drywall, and fit it into the area you want to cover. Secure it in place with four screws, or cover the seams with molding to trap the panel in place. Attach the molding using screws so it can be removed.

1. *When preparing for an access panel, be sure all edges of the access panel will be backed by a framing member. Here a short horizontal two-by has been added between stud bays for just this reason.*

2. *Install drywall all the way around the area that will be covered with an access panel. Leave half a stud width exposed around the hole so that the access panel can bear on framing members or blocking along all of its edges.*

3. *Install an access panel using screws, and leave their heads exposed so that the panel can be removed to allow for work on utilities within the wall. If an access panel will be in view, trim it out with molding. Attach the trim boards using screws so that they can be easily removed without damaging either the trim or the drywall.*

Chapter 5

Installing Drywall

So far, you've been selecting materials, gathering tools, and preparing wall and ceiling surfaces. Now comes the main event. Like other facets of the drywalling job, hanging panels has its own time-saving tips, special applications, and unique tools—such as deadmen, panel lifters, and stilts. These may sound like parts of a circus act, but they all prove useful for moving and installing gypsum drywall.

*O*nce you position a panel, whether on a ceiling, a wall, or a tricky place such as a cathedral ceiling, it's critical that you place screws or nails in patterns that will hold it securely and not allow it to sag. You'll need to know how to fasten any drywall configuration you're likely to encounter, from outside and inside corners to curved walls to irregular borders where gypsum meets masonry.

Hanging Tips & Techniques

USING A DEADMAN

A deadman is a temporary brace made of two lengths of 2×3 or 2×4 joined together and braced to form a T. Cut one of these as long as the ceiling is high plus 1 inch (but minus 1½ inches for the crosspiece) and the other about 3 feet long. When hanging ceiling drywall, wedge the deadman beneath a panel to hold it until it can be fastened. These props are especially useful on longer pieces (over 8 feet).

A panel lifter enables one person to adjust the height of the panel yet keep his or her hands free for driving screws or nails.

You may find it necessary to use two deadmen on a ceiling panel, especially if you're working alone. If so, oppose the angles of the two uprights; tilting them the same way creates an unstable situation.

USING A PANEL LIFTER

A panel lifter, either store-bought or shop-built, will raise a panel just 1 inch or so off the floor. You'll use this handy device when installing wall panels nearest the floor. (Floor-level panels are not installed resting on the floor, but rather an inch or so above it. Baseboard trim or heating units will cover the gap.) It's easiest in this situation to lift the panel with your foot by pressing on a simple lever with a lip on one end that tucks under the panel. A panel lifter also gives you fairly precise control when positioning the wallboard, especially if the panel above is set.

If you don't want to buy a panel lifter, make one as described in Chapter 2 (page 33).

USING A STEPLADDER

Stepladders are made from three different materials: wood, aluminum, and fiberglass. Drywallers tend to prefer aluminum for its low cost and light weight. Ladders are rated according to the weight they can safely hold, and by law they must carry a sticker that displays this rating. Type III (light-duty) ladders can support 200 pounds per rung; Type II (medium-duty), 225 pounds; Type I (heavy-duty industrial), 250 pounds; and Type IA (extra heavy-duty), 300 pounds. For most residential work, a Type II will

A deadman can be used for support by wedging it between the floor and the underside of the drywall panel.

A rolling scaffold is an ideal work platform for installing and finishing drywall on walls over 8 ft. and on cathedral ceilings.

serve you well. Keep in mind, however, that drywall is heavy, and if you weigh 200 pounds and lift a 54-pound ¹⁄₂-inch panel, you'll be stretching the limit of a Type II ladder.

A stepladder works best in situations where you have to take care of a single task in one elevated location. Unfortunately, it won't suffice for working on long joints or driving long rows of screws—you'll have to keep getting off the ladder and moving it over. For those jobs, you'll need a scaffold, a step-up bench with a wide top trestle, or planks laid safely over sawhorses.

USING A SCAFFOLD

A scaffold, preferably mounted on casters, provides a versatile support from which to position, fasten, tape, finish, or paint drywall. It provides a wide, long, level platform that adjusts to the desired height. For small-scale jobs, you probably can get by working from a stepladder or step-up benches with wide top planks. For larger jobs, it might be worthwhile to rent a rolling scaffold, which costs relatively little.

Safe Scaffold Checklist

- All open sides and ends of platforms more than 10 feet above the ground must have (as a minimum) 2x4 top rails at 42 inches, 2x4 middle rails, and 4-inch-high toe boards.

- If workers will be passing beneath the scaffold, a screen or net must be stretched between the top rails and the toe boards.

- Lay planks close enough to each other to prevent tools and materials from falling through.

- Planks must be stamped "scaffold plank grade" by an accredited grading agency (such as the Southern Pine Inspection Bureau).

- Planks must extend at least 6 inches but no more than 12 inches beyond the last support.

- If someone may possibly be working above or below you, install planks above and below for safety.

USING A STEP-UP BENCH

By modifying a sawhorse with a wide top plank and side rails that serve as steps, you can create a versatile step-up bench that works well for many drywalling tasks. Simply add a 2×10 plank to the top and two 2×4 or 1×6 side rails as shown in the illustration. You can also rent or buy sawhorses, step-up benches, or trestles that are designed for drywall installation.

A step-up bench or work trestle provides a handy combination short stepladder and work platform for many drywall applications. The height of the trestle should be determined by subtracting your own height from the overall height of the room.

Shoe stilts take some getting used to, and they can be awkward and dangerous, but when mastered they can provide high access and mobility for finishing drywall.

USING SHOE STILTS

Some building codes disallow shoe stilts for commercial contractors, calling them a safety hazard, but if you take the time to get accustomed to them, they are excellent for taping, finishing, or painting drywall. They allow you to move around freely, eliminating the need for scaffolding, sawhorses, and stepladders for at least some parts of the job. The stilts strap to your shoes and calves and can be adjusted for fit. Most rental stores carry them.

USING A DRYWALL JACK

A drywall jack has a steel frame mounted on a central post that sits on a wheel-mounted chassis. You load a single wallboard panel onto the frame. A crank mechanism lets you raise the panel to the desired location on a ceiling and hold it in place for fastening. The frame also tilts up to 90 degrees to position a panel on a high wall. This device will save you a good deal of backwork, and you can find one at just about any equipment rental store.

A panel jack is a real work-saving device when drywalling ceilings. By mounting a panel and lifting it up into position, you have a nearly effortless way to provide ceiling-panel installation.

Screws vs. Nails

For a number of reasons, screws have replaced nails as the dominant fastener used to attach drywall to framing or existing walls. First, you can remove them, in case you should have to pull off a panel for trimming. It's also easier to control a screw's depth, and screwdriving doesn't knock furring strips or studs out of alignment, as hammering does. Screws install more quickly than nails, especially with a self-loading screw gun. Finally, screws simply offer more holding power than nails.

Whether you go with screws or nails, there are three types of each to choose from. (See page 22.) Select Type W screws if you're fastening drywall to wood studs or furring, Type G screws to attach drywall to drywall in a two-layer application, and Type S self-drilling screws if you're fastening drywall to metal studs.

Ringed nails, which have 25 percent more holding power than smooth-shank nails, are used to fasten drywall to wood. Cement-coated nails make use of their coating to add holding power. Cooler nails are used for hanging drywall over rigid insulation.

FASTENING DRYWALL WITH NAILS

Drive nails with a drywall hammer, which has a face that leaves a dimple. When nailing, work across either the length or width of the panel, applying the full schedule of nails as you proceed with each row. Don't nail the perimeter and then the interior. As you work, hold the drywall panel flush against the furring

Screws vs. Nails. *Screws offer more holding power than nails, but skilled use of the drywall hammer still has its place.*

or studs. Don't expect the final hammer blows to miraculously drive the panel tight against the framing.

Keep at least a ³⁄₈-inch margin between the edge of the wallboard and each nail. If you're not using an adhesive, position nails 7 inches apart on ceiling panels and 8 inches apart on wall panels. With an adhesive, you can space them every 16 inches or so on ceilings or walls.

When fully driven, the nailhead should sit in a dimple about $1/32$ inch deep but shouldn't tear the face paper. Make this dimple with the last blow of the hammer. (If you're having trouble with nails popping out, you can try double-nailing the panels instead. See "Fixing Popped Nails or Screws," pages 127–128.)

The dimple created by the head of a hammer when driving drywall nails should be approximately $1/32$ in. deep.

A properly driven nail leaves the paper face undamaged and has the best holding power.

An improperly driven nail, which has punctured the paper face and entered the core, offers little holding power.

This nail, driven in at an angle, still shows damage to the face, creating a weakened connection.

FASTENING DRYWALL WITH SCREWS

Drive screws with a variable-speed drill and Phillips-head driver, or use a self-feeding screw gun. As with nails, work across the length or width of the panel. Never screw the entire perimeter and then the interior. As you work, hold the panel flush against the framing. If there is a gap between the drywall and the studs, the screw will sink through the panel instead of drawing it tight against the studs.

Again, keep each screw at least $^3/_8$ inch in from the edge of the panel. Position screws along each edge and each framing member, spacing them every 12 inches for ceilings and 16 inches for walls.

When using adhesives on ceilings in which the panels lie parallel to the joists or furring, apply screws every 16 inches along the edges and 24 inches along frame members.

If the panels lie perpendicular to framing, apply screws every 16 inches on the ends and edges and either 16 or 24 inches on the interior, depending on the frame spacing.

When using adhesives in wall applications, space screws (both horizontally and vertically) to match the stud spacing, whether the panels lie perpendicular or parallel to the framing.

If possible, drive drywall screws using a screw gun, which has an adjustable clutch. The clutch can be set to drive the screw to the appropriate depth, at which point it will disengage. Make sure that you drive screws squarely into the panels. Driving them at an angle will tear the paper, which makes finishing more difficult, reduces the screws' holding power, and limits the sheer strength of the panel.

Fastening with Nails

Drywall attached to framing with nails but without adhesive demands a maximum 7-in.-on-center fastener spacing on ceilings and a maximum 8-in.-on-center fastener spacing on walls.

Drywall attached to framing with nails and heavy-duty construction adhesive reduces the requirement to a maximum 16-in.-on-center fastener spacing on both ceilings and walls.

Fastening with Screws

Drywall screwed to framing without adhesives demands a maximum 12-in.-on-center fastener spacing on ceilings and a maximum 16-in.-on-center fastener spacing on walls.

Drywall screwed to ceilings (parallel to the joints) with adhesive cuts the demand to a maximum 16-in.-on-center spacing along its edges and 24-in.-on-center fastener spacing in its interior.

Drywall screwed to ceilings (perpendicular to the joists) framed 16 in. on center with adhesive demands a maximum 16-in.-on-center fastener spacing. Drywall screwed to walls framed 16 in. on center with adhesives demands a maximum 24-in.-on-center fastener spacing.

Drywall screwed to ceilings framed 24 in. on center with adhesive demands a maximum 16-in.-on-center fastener spacing along its edges, and 24 in. on center in its interior. Drywall screwed to walls framed 24 in. on center demands a maximum 24-in.-on-center fastener spacing.

The Pros Know

Do-it-yourselfers normally use drywall nails and a hammer to hang gypsum drywall. Most pros favor screws and a power screw gun because it's faster and easier, and the screwheads leave dainty little dimples that are easy to finish.

But you can use both—on the same sheet. Carrying a power tool that's loaded down with batteries or trailing an electrical cord gets in the way, at least until the sheet is fastened and you have both hands free. So you can pound in enough nails to hold the panel in place, and go back later to fasten the remainder of the panel with power-driven screws.

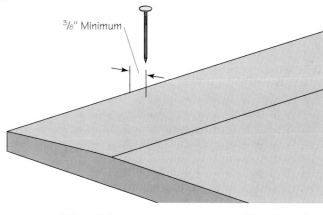

Fastening Edges. Drive fasteners no closer than ³/₈ in. from the panel's edge to prevent the edge from splitting or tearing.

Wrong

Correct

An overdriven drywall screw, left, has torn the drywall panel's face paper. A properly driven screw, right, has its head sitting just beneath the surface of the face of the drywall, but not driven so far that it tears the face paper.

Hanging Drywall on a Ceiling

A ceiling installation generally requires two people, preferably three, and should always be done before the walls. With a three-person crew, two can hold the panel in place while the third drives the fasteners. If you have a two-person crew, both workers will hold the panel in place as they fasten.

One person can hang a ceiling, but it takes skill and patience. If you intend to try it, temporarily nail 2×4s on the top plates, leaving just enough space for the panels ($\frac{1}{2}$ inch, $\frac{5}{8}$ inch, or whatever thickness you're using). Using these blocks and a deadman or two, you can probably handle the job solo if you can't find any helpers.

As with any drywall job, choose longer panel lengths to reduce the number of joints. Install the longest panel you can handle. If your ceiling measures 10 × 12 feet, use three 4 × 10-foot panels rather than three 8-foot panels (with patches to fill in the gaps). This will reduce the amount of finish work substantially. (See "Laying Out a Drywall Job," pages 40–43, for solutions.)

Hanging Drywall on a Ceiling. Always take care not to hurt your neck or your lower back when hanging ceiling panels.

Tools and Materials

Difficulty Level: 🐾🐾

- Drywall panels
- Measuring tape
- Chalk-line box
- Utility knife
- Sawhorses and planks or scaffolding
- Screw gun
- Drywall screws (or nails)
- Permanent marker

1. MAKE THE NECESSARY CUTS ON THE DRYWALL, AND MARK THE JOISTS.

Cut a drywall panel to size, and then cut holes for utility boxes, pipes, and ductwork, as explained in Chapter 4, beginning on page 63. After cutting, mark the joist locations on the top plate with a permanent marker so that you'll be able to find them after you've positioned the panel. Rest the panel so that the face side will face downward when it is picked up and put in place against the ceiling joists or furring. Position your scaffold or sawhorses and planks parallel with the long edge of the panel (generally, perpendicular to the joists). This will provide solid footing and a sturdy work surface along the full length of the panel.

2. APPLY ADHESIVE TO THE STUDS.

If required, apply adhesive to the joists or furring. Even if you have two workers, you may want to nail 2×4s to the top plate (as recommended on page 83 for solo installation).

3. POSITION THE FIRST PANEL.

With a helper, pick up the panel, and tuck one side into the corner where the ceiling and wall meet. With this end of the panel positioned, push the other end into place. If it binds, the panel needs to be trimmed—don't force it. If the panel fits properly, move on to Step 4.

4. FASTEN THE PANEL IN PLACE.

With the panel in position, hold it flush against the furring or joists. (Two workers can support it with their heads. However, this can put a kink in your neck, particularly if you turn from side to side under the panel's weight. To ease the strain, keep movements to a minimum, and remove the head support once you've driven six or seven fasteners.) Fasten the panel in place using screws or nails, following the schedules presented earlier in this chapter. Continue toward the opposite corner in this way, butting each new panel tight against the previous one.

1. *The location of the ceiling joists should be marked on the top plate, so they can be easily found after the panel is lifted into place.*

2. *Apply adhesive to each joist to be covered by the panel.*

3. *Two people can easily move the ceiling panel into position, but have fasteners ready once the panel is snug against the joists.*

4. *Keeping the panel tight against the joists, attach nails or screws according to the ceiling fastener schedule.*

The Pros Know

With a crew of three, let the drywall-cutter start a row of nails along the edge of the sheets that will butt against the ceiling before they are fitted into place. The sheets arrive in place ready for several quick hammer blows, and everyone holding the sheet can let go. It works well along the ceiling, where the cutter doesn't have to measure 16-inch centers to start the nails over studs. A rough estimate is fine because of the double 2x4 plate that's usually above the studs.

5 Installing Drywall

Hanging Drywall on a Flat Wall

Attaching panels to a flat wall goes more quickly than to a ceiling. However, lifting and positioning the top row (or rows) still takes a good deal of energy and planning. It's only when you get to the bottom row that the job becomes relatively easy. Whether you're covering a ceiling or a wall, the same principles apply:

◥ Install the largest panel you can handle.

◥ Hold the panel firmly against the framing before fastening it in place.

◥ When sizing a panel, cut it small enough to fit without binding but large enough that it doesn't leave a gap too wide (more than about ¼ inch) to be taped and filled easily.

Hanging Drywall on a Flat Wall.
Two people can hang wall panels with the greatest of ease.

Tools and Materials

Difficulty Level:

- Drywall panels
- Measuring tape
- Chalk-line box
- Utility knife
- Adhesive and caulking gun
- Screw gun
- Drywall screws (or nails)
- Panel lifter

1. PREPARE THE PANEL, AND APPLY ADHESIVE.

Cut a drywall panel to size, and then cut holes for utility boxes, pipes, and ductwork, as explained in Chapter 4, beginning on page 63. Rest the panel so that the face side will face outward when you pick it up and position it on the wall. If required, apply adhesive to studs or furring.

2. PLACE THE PANEL ON THE WALL.

As a rule, hang the top row first. With a helper, pick up the panel, and place it firmly against the stud wall. Check to see that the drywall covers just half of a stud face it will share with another panel. If necessary, rest an upper panel on nails driven into the studs until you secure it in place.

3. FASTEN THE DRYWALL TO THE STUDS.

Apply pressure to the panel to ensure full contact with framing members, and then screw or nail it in place using the schedules presented earlier in this chapter.

4. BUTT THE LOWER PANEL UPWARD.

Once you've installed the top row of panels against the ceiling, push the lower rows against them using some type of panel lifter. Remember, it's okay to leave a gap along the bottom at floor level—base molding will cover it.

1. *After cutting the panel to size, apply construction adhesive to the face of studs with a caulking gun.*

2. *Wall panels should be raised upward, against the ceiling or the wall panel above it.*

3. *The drywall panel should be pressed firmly against the studs before attaching nails or screws. By driving two nails into the bottom edge of a drywall panel once it is positioned, you can hold it in place long enough to get the fasteners driven.*

4. *A pry bar and block (or panel lifter) is an ideal tool for fine-tuning panel elevation on the floor level.*

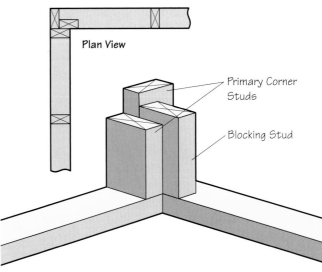

True Corner

Plan View

Primary Corner Studs

Blocking Stud

Hanging Corners and Angles. Inside corners need to have a nailing base for both panels as part of the framing; otherwise, blocking or drywall clips must be added.

Hanging Corners & Angles

HANGING DRYWALL AT AN INSIDE CORNER

Drywall panels can meet at an inside corner (either wall to wall or wall to ceiling) or an outside corner.

At inside corners, framing members must provide a nailing surface for drywall panels that meet there. The illustrations at upper right show two common variations: one for a true corner (where main walls meet) and one for a midwall corner (where a partition wall joins a main wall).

Once you cut the drywall to size and position it, you screw or nail it to the framing in the same manner, regardless of the type of studs used. The fact that a drywall edge meets in an inside corner does not change its fastener treatment, unless you want to create a floating corner. (See "Creating a Floating Corner," page 91.)

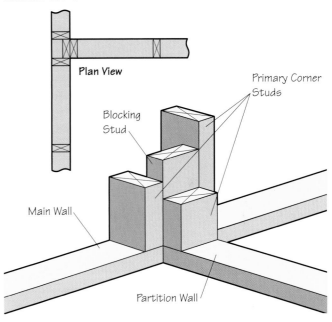

Midwall Corner

Plan View

Primary Corner Studs

Blocking Stud

Main Wall

Partition Wall

When framing a corner, a stud must be in place along both walls to present a nailing surface to the edges of the drywall. This entails adding a blocking stud, as shown in these two drawings.

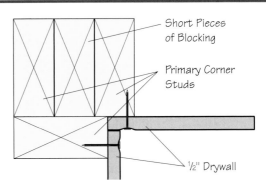

Short Pieces of Blocking

Primary Corner Studs

½" Drywall

Plan view of alternative corner configuration, showing a common arrangement to create a corner, with drywall in place.

2x8 Ceiling Band Joist

2x4 Top Plates

Blocking is missing.

Drywall Clip

½" Drywall Panels

Drywall Clips. In the absence of a 2x4 nailer, drywall clips can be used. They can offer adequate support. In the example to the left, set the clip flush to top of the upper top plate using drywall nails. Install the ceiling panel first as you normally would.

Aluminum-Frame Window

½" Exterior Plywood

2x4 Studs

½" J-Bead

½" Drywall

½" Drywall

J-bead is used to cover and finish the edge of a drywall panel that abuts a nondrywall surface, such as a window or door jamb.

Hanging Drywall at an Inside Corner. At the corner, both walls have a stud for attaching the drywall. This is a sign of a good framing job. Use a panel lifter or lever to snug the lower panel against the upper sheet.

USING DRYWALL CLIPS

Occasionally, you'll find an inside corner that is not framed in such a way that it presents a nailing surface. Nevertheless, panels meeting at corners must have a solid backing, so you'll need to install an extra stud. In cases where this is impossible, you can install drywall clips. These metal 90-degree angles have raised points on one face that are driven into the stud. To attach panels to the clips, use Type S drywall screws, driving them through both the drywall and the clip face.

USING J-BEAD ON AN INSIDE CORNER

Where a drywall panel meets a nondrywall surface on an inside corner, use J-bead to finish the edge. This metal or plastic angle has a lip along one edge

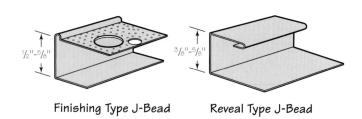

½"–⅝"

⅜"–⅝"

Finishing Type J-Bead

Reveal Type J-Bead

Two types of J-bead: finishing type and reveal type. Finishing type (left) has a front flange designed to be finished with joint compound. The flange on the reveal type J-bead (right) is meant to be left exposed, and requires no finishing.

that wraps around and covers the edge or end of the drywall panel. J-bead comes in either a finishing type or a reveal type. Make sure you match the J-bead size to your drywall thickness: ⅜-inch J-bead for ⅜-inch panels, and so on.

The finishing type resembles corner bead, in that you can finish it in place using joint compound. It has a raised bead that guides the finishing knife as it smooths a layer of joint compound over the exposed lip. You screw this type of J-bead in place before installing a panel in an inside corner. On an outside corner, fit the J-bead onto the drywall edge, and screw it in place after you've installed the panel.

The reveal type is meant to be left exposed. Its front lip has a finished face that presents a completed trim. You can screw this type in place before installing the panel, and then insert the drywall edge into the J-bead. Fasten the panel along its length, but don't screw or nail through the outer lip.

USING L-BEAD

L-bead provides an edge treatment in areas where a drywall panel abuts nondrywall paneling, wood trim, or a door or window casing. As its name implies, L-bead has one face that is slightly wider than the other. The narrower face has a factory finish and needs no joint compound or fasteners, and the other face (like corner bead) consists of perforated galvanized steel with a raised bead. You'll nail this face into the drywall and finish it with three coats of joint compound.

To install L-bead, first screw or nail the drywall in place, leaving a $^1/_8$-inch reveal along its leading edge (the one that meets the paneling, trim, or door/window casing). Next, lay the L-bead in place with the finished face covering the leading edge of the drywall and the perforated face resting on the drywall surface. Screw or nail the perforated face every 5 or 6 inches, and then cover it with joint compound, using the raised bead as a guide for your knife. You don't need to tape this edge treatment, but it does require three coats of joint compound.

Hanging an Outside Corner. Outside corners require metal or plastic accessories to keep the corners strong and sharp.

HANGING AN OUTSIDE CORNER

On walls that form an outside corner, install one panel flush with the outside edge of the corner stud. Attach the adjoining panel so that it overlaps the edge of the first, creating a clean, square corner.

All outside corners require a corner bead, which is screwed in place and then finished with joint compound. Attach the bead with nails spaced every 5 or 6 inches, or set it in place with a corner crimper with the same spacing. Use the proper flange width for your drywall: $1^1/_4$ inch for $^5/_8$-inch panels or $1^1/_8$ inch for anything thinner.

For half-height partition walls, box in the top of the stud wall with a piece of drywall that overlaps the two side panels. Then attach the corner bead, and finish it with joint compound as you would on any other outside corner.

Screw or nail every 5"–6".

Joint Compound

L-bead. *Because of its shape, L-bead can be installed after the drywall is secured in place.*

Screw, nail, or crimp every 5"–6".

Typical 2x4 Outside Corner Configuration

Joint Compound

Metal corner bead *is an essential component of any outside corner. Fasten every 5 to 6 in. to secure it in place. The corner bead will be finished with joint compound.*

USING J-BEAD ON AN OUTSIDE CORNER

Where a drywall panel forms an outside corner that requires trim, J-bead can be used to create a clean edge. In this case, you friction-fit the J-bead onto the drywall edge before installation. Once you've positioned the panel, drive screws or nails through the J-bead and panel (or panel and J-bead if you're using reveal-type J-bead) into the stud.

Wooden Trim

Finishing-Type J-Bead

Screw or nail every 4"–5".

Joint Compound

Outside corner J-bead must be applied to the edge of the drywall before the panel is installed. Fasten it every 4 to 5 in.

CREATING A SCULPTURED EFFECT

You can create sculptural reliefs (geometric or free-form) on walls and ceilings using layers of drywall. Fasten the drywall using adhesive and laminating screws.

Tools and Materials

Difficulty Level:

- Drywall panels
- Measuring tape
- Chalk-line box
- Utility knife or saw
- Caulking gun, adhesive, and laminating screws
- Special corner tape and joint compound

1. LAY OUT THE RELIEF AREA.

Using a chalk line for geometric areas or a pencil for free-form shapes, define the area you want to laminate. You can create stepped soffits on ceilings or decorative areas on walls.

2. INSTALL THE PANELS.

Cut the shapes out using a utility knife or saw. Apply adhesive, and attach them with laminating screws.

3. COVER THE EDGES.

Apply flexible corner tape (available from drywall manufacturers in thicknesses to match the drywall you're using), and finish with joint compound. (See "Taping an Outside Corner," page 112.)

1. Mark out the area you want to laminate on the ceiling or wall. For straight designs, use a chalk line or straightedge and pencil.

2. Cut drywall to the shape and size you need using a utility knife. Secure the pieces in layers using adhesive and laminating screws.

3. Create sharp edges using flexible corner tape and joint compound. The tape comes in sizes to fit different thicknesses of drywall.

HANGING A SLOPED CEILING

Where a knee wall meets a ceiling, an obtuse angle is formed. Drywalling this juncture calls for the same principles as drywalling a regular ceiling, except that holding the panels in place requires ingenuity and, preferably, a drywall jack. Cut and install panels as you would on any normal ceiling, and follow the ceiling screw or nail schedules discussed earlier.

Because a drywall jack can be tilted to match a sloped ceiling, it will save you a great deal of work on this type of installation. In fact, a jack can make it a one-person job, whereas you'd normally need two assistants to hold the panel in this awkward position while you drive the fasteners.

CREATING A FLOATING CORNER

Because corner junctures are the first to *deflect* (the engineer's term for structural movement) as a building adjusts to moisture levels in the framing or to loads added to the structure, the drywall joints are the first to crack. Ironically, proper attachment of drywall with the full complement of screws or nails only aggravates the cracking. The more thoroughly the panels are attached, the more likely they are to move, crack, and gap along with the framing.

Hanging a Sloped Ceiling. *A panel lifter with a tiltable frame simplifies your work. Using this tool, one or two people can install a panel.*

To ease this problem, avoid fastening one of the two drywall panels along the juncture. This solution, known as a floating corner, calls for no fasteners within 7 or 8 inches of the corner. The fastened panel holds the loose edge in place, allowing it to move and reducing the likelihood of cracking.

CREATING A FLOATING WALL CORNER

The Pros Know

If your house has a truss-built roof, be aware that the bottom chord can sometimes arch upward due to variations in moisture content between the top and bottom of the chord. To keep the ceiling panels from pulling away from the wall, don't fasten them at the corner; instead, attach them to a drywall clip on the wall, and don't fasten the clip to the bottom of the truss.

Tools and Materials

Difficulty Level: 🐢

- ◾ Basic hand tools
- ◾ Drywall panels
- ◾ Measuring tape
- ◾ Chalk-line box
- ◾ Utility knife
- ◾ Sawhorses or scaffolding
- ◾ Screw gun
- ◾ Drywall screws or nails

1. INSTALL THE FIRST WALL PANEL.

Frame walls as you would on any standard corner, providing a nailing base for the edges of all panels. Install a panel in one corner, but fasten it only to within one stud bay of the inside edge. Don't fasten this edge to the corner stud.

2. INSTALL THE ADJOINING PANEL.

On the adjoining wall, install the panel with a full schedule of screws or nails, trapping the first panel in place. Fasten this second panel to the corner stud as you would normally.

1. *Fasten the first panel in the usual manner, but leave out the fasteners on the edge at the corner.*

2. *Fasten the second panel, trapping the unfastened corner of the first panel in place.*

Corner Wall Configuration
Plan View

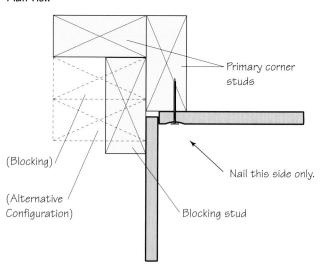

Primary corner studs

(Blocking)

Nail this side only.

(Alternative Configuration)

Blocking stud

In floating corners where walls meet, the framing is standard, but the drywall panels from the opposing walls simply abut, with only one side being fastened to a corner stud.

CREATING A FLOATING CORNER IN A CEILING-WALL JOINT

Tools and Materials

Difficulty Level:

- Drywall panels
- Measuring tape
- Chalk-line box
- Utility knife
- Sawhorses and planks or scaffolding
- Screw gun
- Drywall screws

1. PREPARE THE SURFACE FOR INSTALLATION.

Check the framing members of the wall and ceiling as you would for any standard drywalling job. Make sure to provide a nailing base for both the wall and ceiling panels by adding blocking or drywall clips where necessary.

2. INSTALL THE CEILING PANEL.

Install a ceiling panel in the corner, but fasten it only to within 7 inches of the corner. Do not use any fasteners on the edge adjacent to the wall.

3. INSTALL THE WALL PANEL.

Install the adjoining wall panel, butting it against the ceiling panel as tightly as possible. Fasten it only to within 8 inches of the ceiling corner. The wall panel will trap the ceiling panel in place. Finish the floating joint as you would a normal joint.

Installing Drywall on a Steel-Framed Wall

Although it is still uncommon, more houses are being built with steel framing every year. Installing drywall on steel studs is somewhat different from the method for wooden framing. For more information about steel framing (such as how to add blocking), see "Steel Framing Systems" in Chapter 3, pages 57–58. Remember to use bugle-head Type S screws with self-tapping points to install the drywall—ordinary Type W screws can drill through the 20-gauge steel of non-load-bearing steel studs, but drilling them in will dig out a hole in the drywall larger than the head of the screw, creating finishing problems and unstable drywall.

1. *Floating corners in ceilings that have been furred work the same way as floating corners in walls. First, prepare a nailing base.*

2. *The ceiling panel is installed. Nails should be kept 7 in. from the edge of the panel.*

3. *The wall panel is fastened in place. Nails should be kept 8 in. from the top edge of the panel.*

Steel-Stud Wall Plan View

Install screws close to the web of the stud.

Install this panel first, fastening the entire edge to the open side of the stud.

Attach this panel second, installing all of the screws along the vertical edge of the web side of the stud, and then work toward the other end of the panel.

The open side of all studs in the wall must face in the same direction.

Open Side

Web Side

When installing drywall on steel-stud framing, *always attach panels on the open side of the stud first.*

5 Installing Drywall

Tools and Materials

Difficulty Level: 🔨

- ◼ Drywall panels
- ◼ Measuring tape
- ◼ Chalk-line box
- ◼ Utility knife
- ◼ Sawhorses or scaffolding
- ◼ Screw gun
- ◼ Bugle-head self-tapping screws

1. DETERMINE THE STUD ORIENTATION.

The open side of the C-shaped steel studs should all be facing in the same direction. You should install the drywall along a wall toward the open side of these channels. If you install the panels in the opposite direction—to the solid side first and then the open side—the open end may deflect outward, causing the panels to abut unevenly.

2. INSTALL THE FIRST PANEL.

Install the first wall panel in a corner, as you would for regular wood-framed installation. Begin fastening the screws at the edge away from the corner. At this edge, the screws should be driven in closer to the open side of the stud to allow for the adjacent panel to be installed. In the middle of the panel, drive screws as close to the solid side of the stud as possible, using the Type S screw schedule on page 82.

3. INSTALL THE NEXT PANEL.

Next, attach the abutting panel, and fasten the screws in the same way: starting at the far edge and then working your way back to the joint.

1. Drywall must be installed toward the open side of the steel studs. Check the spacing to ensure panels will have backing.

2. Begin in a corner, fastening screws on the side of the panel away from the corner first, and close to the open part of the stud.

3. Abut the next panel, and fasten it in the same way you did the previous panel: far end first. Here, the installer is finishing up.

Hanging a Curved Wall

Curved walls usually are hung with flexible ¼-inch-thick panels that are designed specifically for such applications (and thus require no special preparation). As an alternative, you can dampen or slit thicker panels as directed below. Curved walls require horizontal installation of panels. For dampened panels, you should avoid cutting out for utilities until the panel has been installed and allowed to dry thoroughly (24 hours). (Mark their location on the floor, and note their heights and dimensions.)

Before you think about hanging panels, you'll probably need to add additional studs. Curved drywall

Concave Side
(This side will be shorter.)

Convex Side
(This side will be longer.)

Hanging a Curved Wall. The concave side of a curved wall is shorter than the convex side—measure both lengths separately. It's best to attach overlong pieces when circumstances allow, and then cut them to size, as these distances are hard to measure.

installation requires closer spacing than the 16- or 24-inch on-center in a typical flat wall. For $\frac{1}{4}$-inch panels, space the studs no more than 6 inches apart; for $\frac{3}{8}$-inch, go with a maximum of 8 inches; and for $\frac{1}{2}$-inch stock, stick with 12 inches. (Avoid $\frac{5}{8}$-inch drywall for this application; it doesn't bend well.)

Note in the illustration above that the inside and outside lengths of a curved wall are not the same. The outside, convex panel has to travel a slightly greater distance than the inside, concave panel. On either side, it's best to cover the curved section with a single panel, because finishing seams on curved walls makes for tedious work. Use over-long panels, and trim them to length after installation. If the curve measures 13 feet, for example, use a 14-foot panel. (You'll end up with slightly more excess on the concave, or inner, side; this makes little difference if you're trimming over-long panels to length, but it can throw you off if you're attempting to cover the curve with shorter pieces that must fit exactly.)

Tools and Materials

Difficulty Level:

- ■ Drywall panels
- ■ Measuring tape
- ■ Chalk-line box
- ■ Utility knife
- ■ Screw gun
- ■ Sawhorses or scaffolding
- ■ Drywall screws
- ■ Plant mister bottle
- ■ Water (a quart for every 4 x 8 drywall panel)

1. CHECK STUD ON-CENTER SPACING.

Double-check the framing to make sure that the maximum stud-to-stud distance does not exceed the spacing recommended for your drywall thickness.

2. WET DOWN THE DRYWALL. (OPTIONAL)

Using a plant mister, spray a quart of water (for a full 4 x 8-foot panel) on the panel side that will be compressed (the face side for a concave wall; the back side for a convex wall). Note: Dampened panels can fall apart, so use at least two, preferably three, people to pick one up. Wait one hour before installation to give the water a chance to soak in.

1. *Check stud spacing to provide proper support for drywall panels. For a single-layer application of $\frac{1}{4}$ in. drywall as shown here, studs should be no more than about 6 in. apart.*

2. *To bend conventional drywall, first mist it with water. A plant mister will serve well for this purpose. In this application, the face side of the drywall panel is being sprayed.*

5 Installing Drywall

3. SLIT THE BACK OF THE PANEL. (OPTIONAL)

As an alternative for concave walls, cut $\frac{1}{8}$-inch deep kerf marks every 2 to 3 inches (or $\frac{3}{4}$ to $1\frac{1}{2}$ inches for $\frac{1}{2}$-inch drywall) in the back side of the panel. (For a very tight radius, it may be necessary to wet *and* slit the panel.)

4. FASTEN THE PANEL TO THE CURVE.

Apply drywall adhesive to the stud edges. With at least one other person, install the drywall panel. Use $1\frac{1}{4}$-inch Type W screws rather than nails. For concave installation, start by screwing the panel to the center studs, and then work toward the end. On convex surfaces, start at one end of the panel, and work your way across.

3. *If necessary for a tight radius, slit the back of the drywall with a utility knife before bending it.*

4. *It takes at least two people to keep a formerly straight piece of drywall tight against a curved wall.*

INSTALLING AN ARCHWAY

The underside of an archway is nothing more than a miniature curved ceiling. You drywall it in much the same way that you'd cover a curved wall, using $\frac{1}{4}$-inch-thick flexible drywall. This material has the flexibility to conform to a fairly small radius without cracking, and it doesn't require dampening or slitting. (If a single layer doesn't provide enough thickness for your wall design or doesn't come flush with the panels covering the wall, install two layers of it, one atop the other.)

If you can't obtain $\frac{1}{4}$-inch panels or don't want to buy a 4×8-foot sheet (often the smallest unit sold) for one small archway, you can use $\frac{1}{2}$-inch-thick drywall. To use this on any but the gentlest of curves without cracking it during installation, you'll have to dampen the back side and slit it every $\frac{3}{4}$ to $1\frac{1}{2}$ inches across the back, depending on the radius of your arch. (See "Hanging a Curved Wall," beginning on page 94.)

Once you cut the piece to the length and width of your archway, hold it in place, and start fastening it in the center. Then, alternating from side to side, work toward both ends of the piece, fastening it every 6 inches. Check for sags, and add fasteners where necessary. Finish the archway-to-wall joints with flexible vinyl corner bead.

Installing an Archway. *Flexible $\frac{1}{4}$-in. panels should fit in an archway without cracking—if not, wet it down and try again.*

Archways. Whether the top of a curved wall opening or a grandiose entryway, installing arched panels is a challenge.

Recommended Bending Radii for Drywall

These bending radii consider the arc of the curved piece of drywall as part of a circle. (The larger the radius, the shallower the curve.) To estimate your bending radius, you'll have to extend your arc into a full circle (either by measuring or estimating) and then measure the radius from the center of the circle.

Formula for Determining the Radius from an Arc

$$2 \times A \times Y = A^2 + B^2$$

Height or Rise of Chord (A)

4'

8'

Radius (Y)

½ of Chord Length (B)

With some simple math you can easily calculate the radius of a circle. Plugging in the numbers from the example at the right:

$$2 \times 4 \times Y = 16 + 64$$
$$8Y = 80$$
$$Y \text{ (Radius)} = 10'$$

Thickness	Dry	Wet	Special flex panels
¼-inch-thick	5' R.	2–3' R.	1½–3' R.
⅜-inch-thick	7½' R.	3–4' R.	n/a
½-inch-thick	20' R.	4-5' R.	n/a

Hanging Drywall in Tricky Locations

DRYWALLING STAIRWAY WALLS

Stairways present a challenge because they often have angled surfaces, with the added challenge of installing drywall panels over stairs. (If you need to work from a scaffold, clamp one end of wide planks to a stepladder, resting the other end on the stairs.) You can simplify the job by installing as many full panels as possible and then measuring and installing the odd-shaped panels last. The existing full panels will give you two of the three dimensions for each triangular panel, which makes it easy to find the length of the third.

Tools and Materials

Difficulty Level:

- Drywall panels
- Measuring tape
- Chalk-line box
- Utility knife
- Scaffolding or stepladder, planks, and clamps
- Screw gun
- Drywall screws (or nails)

1. COVER THE LARGER AREAS WITH DRYWALL FIRST.

Install as many full panels as will fit on the stairway wall, using the same arrangement (horizontal or vertical) that you've used elsewhere.

2. MEASURE SMALLER, IRREGULAR SHAPES.

With the full panels in place, measure for two of the three sides of each triangular piece that must be cut to fit. Transfer those dimensions onto a full panel using a 4-foot T-square.

3. CUT THE TRIANGULAR PIECE TO FIT.

Once you've transferred the two known dimensions, snap a chalk line (or use a straightedge) to connect the end points and mark the unknown length with a cut line. Cut and install this partial panel as you would any other piece of drywall.

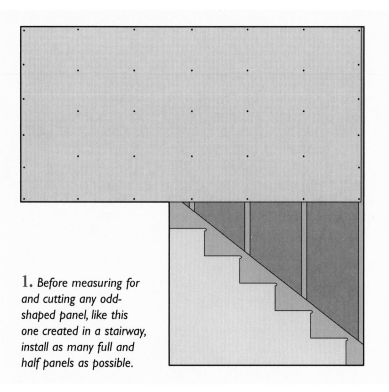

1. *Before measuring for and cutting any odd-shaped panel, like this one created in a stairway, install as many full and half panels as possible.*

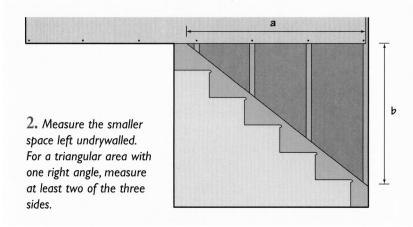

2. *Measure the smaller space left undrywalled. For a triangular area with one right angle, measure at least two of the three sides.*

Hanging Drywall in Tricky Locations.
Drywalling unusual shapes, like triangles and trapezoids, requires extra patience in measuring and cutting, but the hanging is the same.

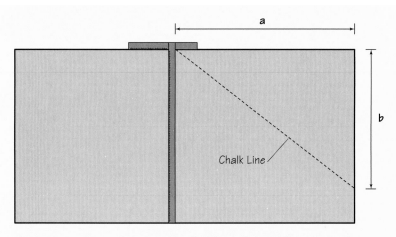

3. *Transfer your measurements onto a full drywall panel, and cut out the irregular shape.*

DRYWALLING CATHEDRAL CEILINGS

Install a cathedral ceiling as you would any other ceiling panel. Use adhesive for a better bond between the panels and rafters, and use the ceiling fastener schedule for nails or screws. Install each panel using a drywall jack, or have two workers stand on stepladders. You'll find that scaffolding is difficult to move around during cathedral-ceiling installation because the drywall jack tends to get in the way. However, scaffolding makes it much easier to finish these panels once you've installed them.

Tools and Materials

Difficulty Level:

- Drywall panels
- Measuring tape
- Chalk-line box
- Utility knife
- Drywall jack
- Screw gun and drywall screws (or nails)
- Stepladder
- Drywall adhesive

1. APPLY ADHESIVE.

If necessary, apply adhesive to the rafter edges or furring. Be careful not to work too far ahead of yourself with the adhesive, as it can set up before you get to that section of ceiling.

2. RAISE THE PANEL USING A DRYWALL JACK.

Place a panel onto a drywall jack. As always, use the largest panel you can handle to minimize finishing work. Raise the jack until the panel makes snug contact with the rafters or furring.

The Pros Know

To prevent cracking at drywall joints where a cathedral ceiling and wall meet, get a strip of metal flashing the length of the joint and 16–20 inches wide. Bend the flashing lengthways to match the wall-to-ceiling angle, and then install it. Fasten only one side. Install the panels on top of the side with the fasteners in the normal way. Then, when you install the other side, screw the drywall through the flashing between studs with Type S screws. Don't screw through the framing members of the roof. This way, any movement in the framing is restricted to one plane instead of to two planes in the drywall joint.

1. *Apply adhesive to the bottom edge of the rafters where you'll be installing the panel.*

2. *When hanging a large cathedral ceiling, a panel lift and a tall sturdy stepladder are two essential tools in the absence of scaffolding. This is at least a two-person job, and it involves moving the stepladder if you are to fully secure the drywall with fasteners.*

3. FASTEN THE PANEL TO THE CEILING.

Move a stepladder into place on one side of the dry-wall jack, being careful not to disturb its base. Working safely from a lower rung, adjust the angle of the jack as needed, making sure that the panel is tight against the framing members. Then fasten the panel to the ceiling using the screw or nail schedule recommended earlier. Work your way across the panel, getting as close to the jack as possible with your ladder. Then move the ladder to the opposite side of the jack and continue fastening. Move the jack away from the wall only when the drywall is entirely fastened. Removing the jack prematurely can lead to sagging in the panel, a problem that is difficult to fix with just screws or nails.

3. *When fastening the panels to the ceiling, it's best to have a helper keep the drywall jack steady.*

DRYWALLING ODD-SHAPED AREAS

Every house seems to have an odd-shaped corner that can't be drywalled with squares, rectangles, or easy-to-figure triangles. The trick is to break down an odd shape into its component lengths or sides, then use a framing square or T-square to transfer the dimensions onto the wallboard. If possible, use a fresh corner or factory edge of the panel for reference in laying out such a piece.

Tools and Materials

Difficulty Level:

- Drywall panels
- Measuring tape
- Chalk-line box
- Utility knife
- 4-foot T-square
- Screw gun
- Drywall screws (or nails)
- Drywall adhesive
- Stepladder

1. MEASURE THE AREA.

Determine the dimensions and angles of the odd-shaped area.

1. *Measure each side of the area you want to fill—drawing yourself a diagram of the shape might be helpful.*

2. MARK THE CUTS ON THE PANEL.

Using a T-square, ruler, or framing square, transfer the dimensions onto a drywall panel. Try to use a factory edge for at least one side of the cutout piece.

3. MAKE YOUR CUTS.

Cut out the piece using a utility knife. If you can't snap this piece cleanly from the panel, score the cut lines repeatedly with your utility knife to make a clean cut, or use a drywall saw.

4. INSTALL THE PIECE.

Test-fit the piece in the odd-shaped hole. Trim its edges where necessary, and fasten it.

2. *Transfer the odd-shaped piece's dimensions onto a piece of drywall, and try to incorporate any of the drywall panel's factory edges if possible (like this corner seen here, top left).*

3. *Cut out the piece with a sharp utility knife. Snap it back if you can, otherwise keep scoring until you break through.*

4. *Install the odd-shaped piece of drywall, and fasten it in place with at least two nails or screws along each edge, or—for larger panel pieces—the recommended on-center spacing.*

Building a Drywall Box around Utilities or Pipes

In some areas of the house (especially basements), you'll want to cover exposed pipes, utilities, or ductwork with drywall. However, drywall can't be attached directly to such fixtures, so you'll have to build a frame box to provide a nailing base for the panels.

Tools and Materials

Difficulty Level:

- Basic hand tools
- Drywall panels
- Measuring tape
- Chalk-line box
- Utility knife
- T-square
- Screw gun and drywall adhesive
- Screws or nails for framing and drywall
- 2x4 or 5/4x4 lumber
- Power miter saw

5 Installing Drywall

1. To drywall over a duct, first measure the duct's dimensions.

Building a Drywall Box around Utilities or Pipes. *Hiding ducts has a practical side, but the boxes can also be decorative.*

1. MEASURE FOR YOUR FRAMING.

Decide on the size of the box needed to cover the pipes or ductwork. Remember that the frame itself will make the drywall stand off the pipe or duct by at least 1½ inches. You may want to make a larger box for design purposes—one that would hold recessed lighting, say. Leave sufficient room for sound-attenuating, fireproof blanket insulation, which is required by many local building codes.

2. BUILD THE FRAMING.

Frame around the duct or pipe, making sure that you provide a nailing base for all drywall edges. Use the same on-center spacing recommended earlier for walls. (This will vary according to the panel thickness you intend to use.) Install the insulation when the frame is completed.

3. DRYWALL THE BOX.

Cut and install drywall on the box framing. Use a ceiling screw or nail schedule for all horizontal sections and a wall schedule for the vertical panels. Complete the corners using corner bead.

2. Frame in the duct with lumber so that the drywall will have a solid nailing or screwing base, as with a regular wall.

3. *Attach drywall to the box frame with the same nail or screw schedules you use on walls. When the pipe or duct is boxed in, complete outside corners using corner bead and inside corners using tape and joint compound.*

Hanging Backer Board for Tile

The type of material required as backer board for tile depends on the tile's location and the type of adhesive you will use. If you're using an organic mastic adhesive and the area will not sustain consistent wetting, standard (or water-resistant) gypsum panels may serve the purpose. However, if the area will have to withstand regular soakings (a shower stall, sink surround, or kitchen-sink area), a cement-based backer board is required. This material also works well in dry areas that call for a heavy underlayment, such as a tiled half-wall surrounding a woodstove, where the surface must be fire-resistant.

■ **Product choices:** Cementitious backer board, a portland cement-based product, comes in ½- and ⅝-inch thicknesses. You can purchase 4 × 8-foot stock, but panels typically measure 32 or 36 inches wide by 5 or 8 feet long.

Hanging Backer Board for Tile. Cement-based panels protect the wall from water damage in bathrooms and kitchens.

■ **Framing:** Framing for cement-based backer board must be spaced no more than 16 inches on center. Steel framing must be 20-gauge or heavier.

■ **Vapor barrier:** Because tile can admit some water, a small percentage of which can then pass through the cement panels, the framing needs a vapor barrier to protect it from moisture. Attach 6-mil polyethylene sheeting as a barrier to the framing using a minimum overlap of 2 inches, or staple it to the back face of the panels using galvanized staples.

■ **Fasteners:** Fasteners must be spaced more closely than with typical drywall (8 inches for walls, 6 inches for ceilings). You'll need special fasteners for cement-panel applications. Use 1½-inch 11-gauge galvanized roofing nails or 1¼-inch galvanized-steel screws. Do not use regular drywall nails or screws. These can rust through, causing the backer board to fail. (To estimate fastener quantities, figure on 1½ times the normal drywall-fastener requirement.)

■ **Taping:** Cement-panel joints must be taped in a similar manner to those on regular drywall, although you don't need to finish the joints with trowels and sandpaper. Use tile-setting mortar or tile adhesive instead of joint compound. Tape the joints with a 2-inch-wide polymer-coated, fiberglass mesh tape that is specially designed for cement backer board.

INSTALLING BACKER BOARD

Tools and Materials

Difficulty Level: 🦇🦇

- Measuring tape
- Chalk-line box
- Utility knife
- Cement-based backer board
- 4-foot T-square
- Screw gun
- Staple gun with galvanized staples
- 6- or 10-inch taping knife
- Tile mortar or adhesive
- Vapor barrier (6-mil polyethylene sheeting)
- 2-inch open-mesh polymer-coated tape
- 1¼-inch galvanized-steel screws or 1½-inch galvanized roof nails

1. INSTALL A VAPOR BARRIER.

Fasten the 6-mil polyethylene vapor barrier over the 16-inch-on-center studs. Use galvanized roofing nails or a staple gun with galvanized staples.

2. CUT AND INSTALL BACKER BOARD.

After cutting the cement-based backer board with a utility knife, fasten panels to the studs over the vapor barrier. Space the fasteners 8 inches apart on walls and 6 inches apart on ceilings.

1. *Before you install backer board for tile, you'll need to put up a 6-mil polyethylene vapor barrier on the stud wall to keep the moisture inside the room from getting inside the wall cavity.*

3. FINISH THE JOINTS.

Using tile mortar or adhesive, fill and tape the joints where the backer-board panels meet. Apply a layer of tile mortar, embed the fiberglass mesh tape, and then follow with a wide knife to level the mortar.

2. *Install backer board with nails or screws 8 in. on center for walls, 6 in. on center for ceilings.*

3. *Using tile mortar or adhesive, fill and tape the joints where the backer-board panels meet. Bed the fiberglass mesh tape in a layer of tile mortar or adhesive, and finish using a wide knife.*

Chapter 6

Taping & Finishing

In any drywall job, taping and applying joint compound account for the lion's share of the man-hours. However, this part of the work can also yield the most satisfaction. After the shopping, the planning, and the hard work of installing drywall panels, the final appearance of the job really comes down to how well you apply and finish off joint compound. Sure, it takes practice to tape and finish both quickly and neatly, but within a day or so, you'll find that your technique has developed pretty well. Before long, your work will compare favorably with that of the pros.

*D*uring other phases of the job, drywallers rely on specialty tools to streamline the work. Taping and finishing, however, still call for the same tools that have been around since gypsum drywall was first introduced: wide knives for applying the joint compound and sandpaper for smoothing the joint after it has dried.

Taping joints involves four steps and requires three coats of joint compound. After you've installed and properly fastened the drywall, a rough coat (or tape-embedding coat) goes on first. While this coat is still wet, you press drywall tape into it, and then wipe away the excess joint compound. After this coat has dried, you apply a filler coat over the rough-coated tape, allow it to dry, and then use a wide knife to scrape high spots. Finally, a third coat (the finish coat) covers the entire joint. Once you've smoothed it a bit and feathered the edges, this coat should render the joint invisible beneath a coat of paint.

Taping Prep: A Checklist

◼ Ventilate the room with fans or by allowing a cross-breeze. This will lower humidity and accelerate the drying process.

◼ Double-check all panels to make sure that they're firmly attached.

◼ Verify that cutouts have been made for all outlets, switches, and fixtures.

◼ Assemble tools, joint compound, and tape in one area. Double-check estimates to ensure that you have sufficient joint compound and tape.

◼ Prefill any gap over ¼ inch wide with setting-type joint compound, and then smooth the face of the compound flush with the drywall face. Let this dry entirely before you start the taping procedure, and if necessary, scrape off any high spots.

◼ Clean and remove grit from all taping knives and trowels. Sand their faces smooth if necessary.

Prepare for Taping. *The results of a perfect taping job should be invisible—the seams should be taped and sanded so that no ridges or humps can be seen on the painted wall.*

◼ Position ladders and scaffolds within easy reach.

◼ Make sure the temperature in the room where you'll apply joint compound remains at least 55 degrees F for 24 hours following application.

The Pros Know

Before using joint compound, loosen it up by blending it with a masher. Well-blended joint compound goes on smoothly and—if mixed correctly—shouldn't contain lumps. On the other hand, joint compound that has been over-mixed will be full of air bubbles, which will pop and show up as little indentations when the mud dries. In either case, the only fix is to smooth down the mistake, and start again with a new batch of mud.

Taping Joints on a Flat Wall

Tools and Materials

Difficulty Level:

- 5- or 6-inch knife
- 10- or 12-inch straight-handled knife
- 10- or 12-inch beveled trowel
- Joint compound
- Drywall joint tape
- Stepladder or scaffolding, as required
- 120-grit sandpaper or sanding sponge

1. APPLY THE FIRST COAT.

Using a 5- or 6-inch knife, apply a coat of joint compound to the joints, spreading it evenly to a thickness of about ¼ inch. Cover the entire length of the joint. Make sure that you completely fill any gaps between panels. Note: if you're using fiberglass mesh tape, apply it before the first coat. The compound then oozes through the mesh and binds to the wall.

2. TAPE OVER THE FIRST COAT.

Working with a strip of drywall tape that ideally measures the same length as the entire joint, press the tape into the wet first coat using your fingers, being careful not to create any folds or wrinkles. Make sure that the tape centers on the joint. Using a 5- or 6-inch knife (working from top to bottom on a vertical joint), apply light pressure to the tape, and draw the knife along its full length, squeezing joint compound out from beneath the tape as you smooth the coat. If the tape blisters, you haven't left enough joint compound beneath it. Peel the tape back in just that section; add joint compound to the blistered area; and proceed. You should leave a thin layer of joint compound beneath the tape.

How Drywall Joints Differ

Flush end-butt joints are formed wherever the untapered factory ends of drywall panels meet, where cut edges come together, or where an untapered end joins a factory tapered end. Unlike the joints formed by factory-tapered panel edges, end-butt joints provide no recess for joint compound.

Factory-tapered panel edges provide a recess for drywall compound.

Flush end-butt joints must be carefully feathered to produce a smooth surface.

1. *Using a taping knife, apply a first coat of joint compound, about the width of the knife.*

2. *Embed the drywall tape in the first rough coat of joint compound, and smooth it against the wall with the taping knife.*

3. REMOVE EXCESS JOINT COMPOUND.

Using the same drywall knife, make a final pass over the tape and bedding coat to remove any excess joint compound. Let this coat dry. Before applying the second (filler) coat, use a drywall knife to scrape or knock down any burrs or high spots that you may have missed while the tape-embedding coat was still wet. Take care not to cause gouges. If you do, apply a thin layer of joint compound to this area.

4. APPLY THE SECOND COAT, AND REMOVE EXCESS.

Load a hawk or mud tray with joint compound. Using a 10-inch straight-handled knife, apply a layer of joint compound as wide as the knife. Make it as smooth as you can get it, using repeat passes if necessary. Let the coat dry thoroughly. Again, use a scraper to knock down any burrs or high spots that you may have missed.

5. APPLY THE FINISH COAT.

Using a hawk or mud tray and a 10- or 12-inch finishing trowel, apply a wide finish coat to the taped joint. This should be a light skim coat, not a heavy application. Move with long steady strokes, pulling in one direction and feathering out both edges to create the smoothest possible transition to the drywall face. Sand the joint if necessary.

4. *The 10-in.-wide filler coat can be applied with a straight-handled drywall knife or a finishing trowel.*

3. *Remove the excess mud from the edges around the tape with the same taping knife as before.*

5. *For the finish coat, apply, smooth, and finish wet joint compound using a 12-in. finishing trowel.*

TAPING FLUSH END-BUTT JOINTS

A flush end-butt joint is more difficult to finish than a tapered joint because you have to put more work into feathering the layers of joint compound. Because there's no recess for it to sit in, the joint compound on finished end-butt joints will inevitably form a slight mound. The idea is to make this mound as inconspicuous as possible.

You'll need to feather out the edges of the joint to a greater width, leaving a wider seam than is required for factory tapered joints. A bump that is $1/8$ inch high but 16 to 18 inches wide will seem flat to all but the closest inspections, but a narrower one can still be felt when you pass your hand over it.

Not only do end-butt joints require more work, they also provide slightly less stability than factory tapered joints, which makes them more likely to crack. To compensate for this, use fiberglass mesh tape (which adds strength) rather than paper tape.

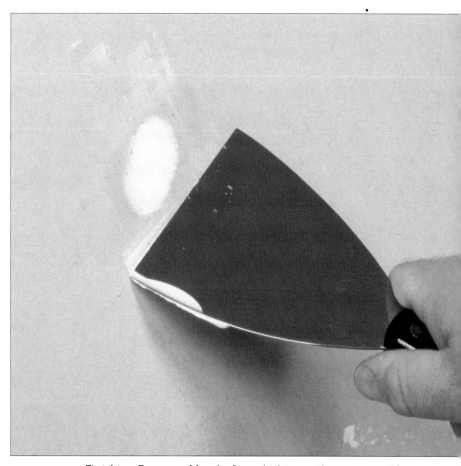

Finishing Fastener Heads. *Properly driven nails or screws, with shallow dimples, make finishing much simpler.*

Finishing Fastener Heads

The dimples left by screw- and nail-heads don't require the same treatment as taped joints. For properly driven fasteners, three coats of joint compound will suffice.

Tools and Materials

Difficulty Level:

- 5- or 6-inch knife
- 10- or 12-inch straight-handled knife
- Joint compound
- Stepladder or scaffolding, as required
- 120-grit sandpaper or sanding sponge

1. APPLY THE FIRST COAT, AND SCRAPE FLAT.

Using a 5- or 6-inch knife, apply a thin swath of joint compound over the fastener heads. This coat should merely fill in the dimple you created by driving or hammering the fastener. Rather than treat them one at a time, you can cover an entire row of them with one pass. This will make the joint compound less conspicuous. Let this first coat dry completely, and then scrape off any burrs or high spots that remain.

1. *Rather than mudding nail- or screw-heads one at a time, you can cover them with long swaths of joint compound.*

2. APPLY A SECOND COAT, AND SCRAPE FLAT.
Apply the second, slightly wider coat of joint compound to the fastener heads using a 10-inch straight-handled knife. Allow this coat to dry completely, and then scrape it smooth.

3. APPLY THE FINAL COAT.
Using a 10-inch straight-handled knife, apply a third coat of joint compound that covers the second coat entirely. Carefully feather the edges, creating a gradual transition to the drywall surface. Allow this coat to dry completely, and sand it if necessary.

2. *A larger swath of joint compound is easier to feather and blend into the face of the drywall panel.*

The Pros Know
A small homemade dolly (about 20 to 24 inches square) fitted with 4-inch casters makes an excellent helper for quickly moving buckets of joint compound around. If you're working off a stepladder or using shoe stilts, you can stack up two or three buckets so you don't have to bend down every time you want to reload your hawk. Construct the dolly strong enough to handle all that weight—three big buckets weigh 180 pounds when full.

3. *The final coat of joint compound should be feathered out so thinly that it appears flat.*

Taping an Inside Corner

Tools and Materials
Difficulty Level: 🦇🦇
- 5- or 6-inch knife
- 10- or 12-inch straight-handled knife
- Inside corner knife
- Joint compound
- Paper drywall tape
- Tape bender
- Stepladder or scaffolding, as required
- 120-grit sandpaper or sanding sponge

1. PREPARE THE DRYWALL TAPE.
Run a length of drywall tape along the inside corner, and cut the tape to size. Run the tape through your tape bender to fold it in half lengthwise. (Or fold it by hand.) Have this tape ready.

2. APPLY THE ROUGH COAT.
Using a 5- or 6-inch knife, apply a 4-inch-wide layer of joint compound to both faces of the inside corner. Make this layer about ¼ inch thick.

3. EMBED THE TAPE AND REMOVE EXCESS.
While the first coat is still fresh and wet, use your fingers to embed the folded drywall tape into the

6 Taping & Finishing

Taping an Inside Corner. Well-filled joints are particularly important at inside corners, which are susceptible to cracking.

compound. Use an inside corner knife or a regular 5-or 6-inch knife to seat the tape, drawing it firmly from ceiling to floor and squeezing out any excess joint compound from beneath the tape. Allow the first coat and tape to dry thoroughly before the next step. Scrape off any burrs or high spots.

1. Paper drywall tape has a slight crease down its center, making it easy to fold in half for use in corners.

2. Apply a rough coat, and embed a length of drywall tape (creased at its center line) the full length of the joint.

3. An inside corner knife enables you to embed the tape and smooth joint compound on both sides of a corner simultaneously.

4. APPLY A SECOND COAT.

Use a 10- or 12-inch straight-handled knife to apply a slightly wider layer of joint compound to each face of the inside corner. Be careful not to let the corner of the knife cut the tape. Feather the edges to the drywall faces. Let this coat of joint compound dry completely, and then scrape off any burrs or high spots.

5. APPLY THE FINISH COAT.

Using a 10- or 12-inch straight-handled knife, apply a top coat to each face of the inside corner. Feather the edges to create a gradual transition to the panel faces. At this point, you may want to use an inside corner knife to form a crisp, straight line where the two walls meet.

4. *Apply a filler coat over the embedded tape. Make this coat slightly wider than the first coat.*

The Pros Know

When taping an inside corner, make sure that the three lengths of tape that meet at the corner (the wall joint and the two ceiling joints) don't have any gaps between them. If the joint is not completely covered by tape, the mud may crack or separate from the corner, leaving a hole.

5. *After the filler coat is dry, spread a finish coat on each face of the corner panels.*

Taping an Outside Corner

Tools and Materials

Difficulty Level:

- 5- or 6-inch knife
- 10- or 12-inch straight-handled knife
- Joint compound
- Stepladder or scaffolding, as required
- 120-grit sandpaper or sanding sponge

Note: This procedure assumes that you've attached corner bead to the outside corner. If not, please refer to pages 89–90 for instructions on installing it.

1. APPLY A FIRST COAT, AND REMOVE THE EXCESS.

Using a 5- or 6-inch taping knife, spread a 4-inch-wide layer of joint compound on each face of the outside corner. Corner bead has a raised edge, or bead, at the 90-degree bend that acts as a screed for your knife, helping you to create an evenly tapered layer of joint compound between the bead and panel face. As you smooth and feather the coat, keep the outermost point of this bead free of joint compound. Let this coat dry thoroughly, and then scrape off any burrs or high spots.

Taping an Outside Corner. Outside corners, at risk to damage, are reinforced with metal or plastic bead before finishing.

2. APPLY A SECOND COAT, AND REMOVE THE EXCESS.

Use a 10- or 12-inch straight-handled knife to apply a slightly wider layer of joint compound to both faces of the outside corner. Smooth and feather the coat to the drywall surface. Allow the coat to dry completely, and then scrape it smooth.

3. APPLY THE FINISH COAT.

Using a 10- or 12-inch straight-handled knife, apply a top coat to both faces of the corner. Feather the edges to make a gradual transition to the faces of the drywall panels, and sand the surfaces if necessary.

2. *No tape is used on an outside corner, but a second filler coat is applied just as it is with any other seam. Corner bead is designed with a raised bead edge at its corner, which supports one end of the edge of the drywall knife and leaves behind an even layer of joint compound.*

1. *After installing the corner bead, coat it with a layer of joint compound on each face of the outside corner's drywall panels.*

3. *Use a wide straight-handled knife to apply a final coat, feathering its edges as you blend it into the face of the drywall panels.*

6 Taping & Finishing

The Pros Know

It's easy to check a drywall joint for excessive crowns or recesses after you've applied the second or third coat of joint compound. Hold the straight edge of a trowel or wide drywall knife across the top of the joint, and see whether you can detect a gap between the joint compound and the ends of the knife. Rock the knife from side to side. If the gap measures more than 1/16 inch or so, you'll need to apply a wider swath of joint compound and feather it out more gradually.

This gap should be no more than 1/16".

Finish-Sanding

Sanding drywall seams involves two steps. Make a first pass using a sanding pole fitted with 120-grit sandpaper. Then hand-sand with 150-grit paper. For this step, fold the sandpaper in quarters, or attach it to a sanding block.

As an alternative to this two-step process, you can sand with a fine screen mounted on a handle, or wet-sand (a dustless approach) using a small-celled polyurethane sponge designed for this purpose. Wet-sanding with one of these sponges does not yield as fine a finish as dry-sanding with 150-grit, but in situations that don't permit dust, it makes a good substitute for the pole-sanding/hand-sanding technique. If you're particularly sensitive to dust (or happen to have the equipment handy), you can use a commercial sanding machine with a wet/dry vacuum attachment for nearly dust-free sanding.

Finish-Sanding. Sanding is labor-intensive, and it produces a lot of dust, but painstaking sanding jobs make the smoothest walls.

You'll find that lighting the work area carefully is essential to good finishing. If you shine light directly on a drywall joint, imperfections may not show up. Move the light to the side of the drywall, or shine it from above or below, and you're more likely to detect creases, recesses, bulges, and other defects. For this purpose, acquire a portable high-powered light source, such as a halogen lamp. Place it on a stand in order to free up both hands, or carry a portable light in one hand and sandpaper in the other as you return to survey the joints and spot-sand any imperfections.

If possible, seal off your work area to keep dust from drifting into finished rooms. To accomplish this, set up a dust barrier of polyethylene sheets between the work space and all clean areas, and seal all four edges with masking tape. Keep in mind that joint-compound dust is very fine-grained and can escape through tiny cracks between doors and jambs or around unsealed dust barriers.

Tools and Materials

Difficulty Level:

- Dust mask
- Hat
- Masking tape
- Dust barriers (polyethylene)
- Portable, high-powered work light
- Dry sanding sponge (if required)
- Pole sander with universal joint
- Sanding block
- Sanding screen
- Safety goggles
- Wet/dry shop vacuum
- 120- and 150-grit sandpaper
- Broom and vacuum cleaner

1. SAND THE JOINTS SMOOTH.

Using a sanding pole loaded with 120-grit sandpaper, sand each of the joints if necessary. Keep edges smooth as you taper them into the face of the drywall. To avoid sanding through the top layers of joint compound and into the tape, apply gentle, even pressure, and resist the urge to bear down. If you do sand through to the tape, mark this area with a pencil, and reapply a coat of joint compound.

2. CHECK FOR IMPERFECTIONS.

Before starting to finish-sand (with 150-grit paper), position your light so that it illuminates the seams you intend to sand. Lighting from the side will cast the light across imperfections and make them evident.

3. FINISH-SAND THE JOINTS.

Using folded 150-grit paper, a sanding block loaded with 150-grit paper, a sanding screen, or a urethane sponge—depending on your preference and the job at hand—sand the seams and also the swaths of joint compound that cover fastener heads. Next, run your hand over the area to check for smoothness. On inside corners, where sanding blocks are hard to control, use just a folded sheet of paper for hand-sanding. Vacuum up drywall dust now, before you track it to other rooms and before you remove the dust barrier.

2. *Check the joints for smoothness with the palm of you hand, sanding down any high spots or bumps that you feel.*

1. *A sanding pole is an ideal tool for sanding drywall ceiling and wall seams.*

3. *Hand-sanding may be required to get into corners. Using a sanding pole here may damage the seam.*

Special Finishes. *This room, having been taped, finish-coated, and sanded, is ready for painting or texture finishing.*

Cleaning and Maintaining Taping Tools

Joint compound cleans up easily using only water. By spraying the tools with a hose or a blast of water from a faucet, you can remove all joint compound, wet or dried. Use one knife to scrape another. Note: don't wash joint compound down the drain, as it could form sediment that may clog your pipes.

Once you've cleaned drywall knives, set them out to dry so that water runs off the blades and doesn't have a chance to pool on them. Otherwise, the blades will rust quickly. If they do rust or if you've missed some joint compound, simply sand them clean.

It's critical that you keep knife blades true and free of bends (except for the slight curves you may have introduced to help with crowning). To ensure this, store knives where they won't be bent or bowed beneath the weight of other tools.

Special Finishes

Textured walls and ceilings add a low-tech, inexpensive design feature to any interior. These textures may appear finely wrought and difficult to achieve, but with a little practice, you can successfully imitate the effects of old-world craftsmen. Even better, they can hide some mistakes you may have made when hanging the panels. (And it's not even considered cheating!) Once you've practiced and experimented a bit on scrap drywall, you'll have the skills to texture your own walls or ceilings using basic tools and materials.

No matter what type of texture you intend to apply, you must first complete all joints and fastener heads as described earlier in this book. Although texturing can hide errors, it provides no substitute for proper finish work. Before you texture, finish and prepare all drywall panels just as you would for painting (although there is no need to be as fussy as you would be for a painted wall).

APPLYING SPRAYED FINISHES

Unlike most texturing treatments, blown ceilings and walls require advanced skill and equipment that most people will have to rent. A popcorn-like material (polystyrene or vermiculite) is fed from a hopper to an airless spray gun, which is attached to an air compressor. Once it is blown onto the surface, it is left to dry without retouching. This texturing takes some practice to apply properly, so consider hiring a painting or drywall contractor to do the work for you if you have no experience with it.

Another common treatment is an orange-peel finish. You create this texture by spraying watered-down joint compound through an airless paint sprayer. If left to dry untouched, the surface will resemble that of an orange peel. However, you must add just the right proportion of water, and mastering the spraying technique takes lots of practice. (An orange-peel finish can also be applied by hand.)

Orange-peel texture can be applied with a paint roller (shown before being flattened with the knockdown technique).

APPLYING AN ORANGE-PEEL TEXTURE

If you don't have experience with airless paint sprayers, a number of hand-applied textures will still give you a professional-looking finish. For example, to achieve an orange-peel finish without a sprayer, simply use a paint roller to apply the watered-down joint compound.

If the roller produces the texture you want, allow it to dry as is. However, you may have trouble getting a good orange-peel effect using this approach, especially on inside corners (though this can be achieved with practice and patience). If this is the case, try knocking down the half-dry surface. This usually improves the appearance of this texture, making it more consistent with an orange-peel look.

Sprayed finishes are fed through a hopper into a spray gun. The texturing—a popcorn-like material—is blown onto the surface and left to dry without retouching.

Tools and Materials

Difficulty Level:

- ½-inch-nap roller
- Roller pan
- Water
- Bucket of joint compound, half full
- Mixer or mixing stick
- Test scrap of drywall, approximately 2 x 2 feet
- 18- to 24-inch straightedge or finishing knife
- Stepladder or scaffolding, as required

1. THIN JOINT COMPOUND.

Choose a bucket of joint compound that is at least half full, but not one that is brand-new and filled to the top. Add some water to the bucket of joint compound—you'll need enough to make it spreadable with a roller but not runny. (See next step.)

2. MIX THE THINNED COMPOUND.

Using a hand mixer or a mixing paddle chucked into an electric drill, or by hand, mix the water and joint compound until its consistency matches that of paint or very heavy cream. (If it doesn't seem thin enough, add more water and mix again. If you think you added too much water, add some more undiluted joint compound. Experiment with small batches to derive the right proportion of water to add.)

3. CHECK THE MIXTURE'S CONSISTENCY.

Pour some of the mixture into a roller pan. Using a roller, apply it to a piece of scrap drywall held upright. The mixture should not sag or run. If it runs, add more joint compound; if it turns out to be too thick to roll, add more water.

2. *The easiest way to mix joint compound is to use a mixing paddle and a power drill.*

1. *The joint compound needs to be diluted until it can be rolled on the wall with a paint roller.*

3. *Before applying the texture to the wall, test the joint compound's consistency on a scrap piece of drywall.*

4. ROLL A FIRST COAT ONTO THE WALL.

Using the ½-inch-nap roller, apply the mixture to the wall. Roll it as you would roll on paint, covering every square inch of the wall. Get as close to the corners and edges as possible. Allow this application to dry for 10 minutes or until it loses its shine.

5. ROLL ON A SECOND COAT.

After the first coat has dried, roll on a second coat. Work the roller over the surface until you achieve the desired effect. Make sure that you're satisfied with it, because you shouldn't touch the wall again except to paint it. Wash out the roller with water. Cap the joint-compound bucket, and then date it and label it "orange peel" so you won't mistake it for standard joint compound on future projects.

6. KNOCKING DOWN THE FINISH.

As an alternative, you can modify orange-peel texture to give it a knocked-down look. Holding an 18- to 24-inch rigid straightedge or finishing knife almost flat to the wall, draw it across the half-dry orange peel finish, applying extremely light pressure. Check your work as you go, because the finish you leave will be the final look. You can vary the finish by applying more or less pressure.

5. *After the first coat of joint compound has dried for at least 10 minutes, use the ½-in.-nap paint roller to apply a second coat.*

4. *For a straight-orange peel finish, first apply watered-down joint compound with a ½-in.-nap roller.*

6. *To knock down the texture, draw an 18- to 24-in. straightedge or finishing knife lightly across the surface while it is still wet.*

*A **brocade finish** imitates the look of brocade, a fabric with a raised design.*

APPLYING A BROCADE FINISH

You can create this unusual finish using unthinned joint compound and a flat metal or wooden hand trowel. The finish looks as if someone spread joint compound onto the surface and then flattened it while it was still wet, without swiping across it to smooth it out. This is exactly what you'll do to apply this finish, working in 4-foot-square sections at a time. This treatment is typically used on ceilings.

Tools and Materials	
	Difficulty Level: 🐟
▧ 5- or 6-inch knife	
▧ Hand trowel (metal or wood)	
▧ Mud pan or hawk	
▧ Joint compound	
▧ Stepladder or scaffolding, as required	

1. SPREAD JOINT COMPOUND ONTO THE WALL.

Using a 10- or 12-inch knife, apply a thin coat of joint compound to a 4 × 4-foot area of the ceiling (or wall). Do not try to smooth the joint compound out, but leave it in an irregular pattern with relatively uniform thickness.

2. FLATTEN IT WITH A TROWEL.

Using a drywall knife or hand trowel, flatten the peaks of the wet joint compound by pressing the

trowel against the surface and pulling it squarely away. Do not swipe laterally to smooth out the finish. Work the wet joint compound to your liking at this time; the texture you leave behind with the trowel will remain as the final finish.

1. *Spread a thin layer of joint compound on a small section of wall using a 10- or 12-in. drywall knife.*

2. *Using a small drywall knife, flatten the surface out in small areas, leaving behind a textured pattern.*

A Spanish-style or stucco finish can be made with various tools, such as the paint-graining comb shown here.

APPLYING A SPANISH-STYLE OR STUCCO FINISH

A Spanish-style finish, one that resembles fancy stucco, is simple to achieve and does an excellent job of concealing any imperfections in the wall that you'd like to hide. You just apply an $\frac{1}{8}$-inch-thick layer of joint compound and then make random curved swaths in the wet material with a 5-inch drywall knife. If you'd prefer a broader pattern, use a notched trowel instead; for a narrower pattern, use a paint graining comb or even a regular plastic hair comb. Because this relatively thick layer takes more time to dry, you can work a larger area than those on which you use thinned-out compound.

Tools and Materials

Difficulty Level:

- Mud pan or hawk
- Joint compound
- 5-inch knife, notched trowel, graining comb
- 10- or 12-inch knife (for application)
- Stepladder or scaffolding, as required

1. SPREAD JOINT COMPOUND ONTO THE WALL.

Using a 10- or 12-inch drywall knife, apply a thin layer of joint compound to the ceiling or wall.

2. MAKE STUCCO PATTERNS IN THE WET JOINT COMPOUND.

While the joint compound is still wet, use a 5-inch drywall knife (or notched trowel, paint graining comb, or other tool) to make circular or swath patterns as desired. Overlap the textured areas slightly so that the entire surface is covered.

1. *Because you can work quickly when creating a stucco-style finish, you can apply joint compound to a larger area.*

2. *To achieve stucco-style texturing, use a notched trowel to make curved patterns in the wet joint compound.*

Jab-and-dab techniques can utilize specially made brushes, but even a sponge will leave a pattern in wet mud.

Textured roller covers made for applying paint can be easily used for applying joint compound.

APPLYING BRUSH AND ROLLER TEXTURES

Almost any implement will leave some type of pattern in wet joint compound. Jab-and-dab techniques make use of textured brushes to create distinctive patterns, and you can achieve similar effects using textured rollers. For either of these methods, apply thinned joint compound to the wall or ceiling surface as described for the orange-peel surfaces. Then, while the mixture is wet, you can jab and dab at it with a sponge like the one shown (or a special brush), or you can roll it using a textured roller.

Textured roller sleeves resemble those used for conventional paint rolling, except that they're covered with a pattern of plastic strands or wires. When rolled across wet joint compound, these strands or wires leave behind a random pattern.

Another textured look can be achieved using a textured brush. This tool resembles a two-headed, side-by-side cloth mop. A handle yokes the two heads, making it easy to press the device into the wet joint compound as you move randomly across the surface to create the texturing. Apply it to the same thinned joint compound that you'd use for the orange-peel textured finish. With a smaller brush or even a sponge, you can make smaller patterns, but this will be a lot more labor-intensive and tedious.

The Pros Know

A couple of gallons of wet joint compound is heavy and cumbersome, as anyone who's hoisted a bucket of it knows. If your ceiling joists are spaced more than 16 inches on center or if you've used thinner panels, there's a good chance that the ceiling will start to sag under all that weight. If these conditions exist but your heart is set on a textured ceiling, finish it with a lighter, vermiculite- or polystyrene-based blown texture.

Skim-Coating

Occasionally, you'll encounter a drywalling phenomenon known as ghosting or photographing. These terms refer to when the seams and patches of joint compound show through the layers of paint. This can happen because the joint compound and drywall face paper have different porosities and therefore absorb paint differently. The problem tends to show up most noticeably with gloss paints and in rooms with a lot of natural light.

There are two ways to defeat or reduce photographing. You can take the easy, high-tech approach, and paint the drywall with a primer-sealer. These prod-

Skim-Coating. *A thin coating of watery joint compound can be applied to walls to provide a consistent surface for priming.*

ucts have a high resin content that can even out the different porosities and help hide the seams. If you'd prefer a more traditional method, you can skim-coat the entire wall with a thin layer of joint compound. This will eliminate the problem by ensuring that every square inch has about the same porosity. Skim-coating also helps make new drywall blend in better with old plaster if you're remodeling an older home. Here's how to apply a skim coat using a conventional nap roller.

Tools and Materials

Difficulty Level: 🔨🔨

- ▪ ⅜-inch-nap roller
- ▪ Roller pan
- ▪ Water
- ▪ Joint compound
- ▪ Mixer
- ▪ 18- to 24-inch finishing knife

1. PREPARE THE WALL AND THE JOINT COMPOUND.

Tape, finish, and sand the drywall joints as explained on pages 106–115. (Skim-coating does not take the place of proper finish work.) Thin the joint compound with water to the consistency of paint or heavy cream.

1. *For skim-coating, joint compound needs to be watered down to the texture of paint.*

2. BLEND THE JOINT COMPOUND.

Mix the watered-down joint compound by hand or by using a mixing paddle chucked into an electric drill. Then pour or scoop out this mixture into a roller pan.

3. APPLY THE SKIM COAT.

Roll a thin layer of the new mix onto the wall, just as you would a coat of paint or primer. This thinned mixture will dry quickly, so work just one wall at a time. (A roller cover with a thick nap will give the surface a slight texture; if you want perfectly smooth walls, use the lowest-nap roller cover available, and apply an even thinner mixture.)

4. SMOOTH OUT THE WET SKIM COAT.

As soon as you've rolled out the thinned joint compound, quickly smooth it with broad, continuous strokes of an 18- to 24-inch finishing knife (or the widest knife or trowel that you have available). Work from the top of the wall to the bottom. You can sand out small ridges later, but try to get the skim coat as smooth and consistent as possible using quick troweling strokes of the knife.

3. To defeat photographing (where joint compound absorbs paint differently from drywall), skim-coat the wall by first rolling on a thin layer of thinned joint compound.

2. Thinned joint compound should be mixed thoroughly, either by hand or with power-driven mixing paddles

4. Before the rolled-on drywall compound dries, smooth it with a wide straight-handled finishing knife.

Chapter 7

Drywall Repairs

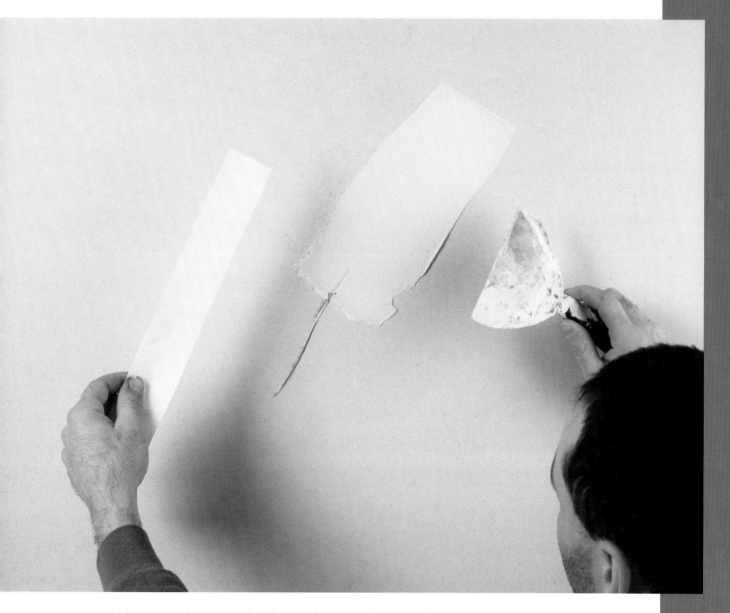

No matter how good a drywall job you do, lots of unavoidable things can happen to create flaws. A new house can settle during its first couple of years, causing cracks to develop in corners or along ceiling joints. In both new and old houses, the moisture level changes seasonally, shrinking window and door frames, pulling the framing away from the drywall panels, and even causing drywall nailheads to pop.

S tructural changes in the house don't get all the credit for drywall damage. A slip of the wrist as you're moving a table can leave a nasty gash. An errant basketball thrown indoors can make a conspicuous dent. How do you fix problems like these? Well, some you can take care of with a little joint compound, a strip of tape, and a sanding sponge. Others may require wood backing or screening.

Troubleshooting

BULGING OR RECESSED DRYWALL

Recessed or bulging drywall can usually be traced to the framing. A misaligned stud stands either *shy* or *proud* of the partition line. In other words, it recedes from or protrudes beyond the plane formed by the row of stud edges that make up a wall.

If the stud is causing a bulge, there's not much you can do to correct it once the drywall has been hung. This problem should have been fixed beforehand by correcting the stud (page 48) or by removing and replacing it with one that aligns properly with the partition line. To hide the bulge at this point, apply an extra-wide (20-inch) layer of joint compound, and feather it out carefully.

If the stud stands shy of the partition line, causing a recess, the problem is relatively easy to fix, provided the stud does not support either end of the drywall panel and the panel is not fastened with adhesive. Before you apply any joint compound, remove the fasteners, or simply drive them all the way through the panel and into the stud so that they no longer hold the drywall against it. Don't drive any additional fasteners; instead, apply joint compound to conceal the old fastener holes.

If the stud coincides with a panel end, then it must have fasteners to support the panel. In this case (or if the panel is fastened with adhesive), build up the recessed joint with multiple and ever-wider layers of joint compound until it comes flush with the rest of the wall.

Bulging or Recessed Drywall

Bulging drywall is usually attributed to a stud that is in front of the stud line (called the partition line), causing a bulge.

Recessed drywall is usually attributed to a stud that is behind the partition line, causing a recess.

Fixing a Bulge

To hide a bulge in a wall, apply an extra-wide band of joint compound across the bulge and carefully feather the edges.

Fixing Recesses

If you have recessed studs that are pulling the drywall out of line, remove (or drive through) the fasteners and apply joint compound over the old fastener holes.

If the recessed stud must have fasteners (if it is a stud at either end of the drywall panel), build up the recess with repeated and ever-wider layers of joint compound until the recess comes flush with the faces of the drywall panels.

FIXING BAD END-BUTT JOINTS

Flush end-butt joints occur where the untapered ends or handmade cuts on drywall panels meet one another. Because the ends don't have the slight taper provided along the factory edges to accommodate the joint compound, these joints tend to bulge once they've been taped and finished. Once you've created these crowns, as they're called, it's difficult to knock them down without sanding through the top layer of joint compound and into the tape beneath. To make an end-butt joint crown less conspicuous, widen the seam of joint compound to about 20 inches, and feather the edges down gradually to the drywall face.

FIXING BROKEN OR BLOWN-OUT DRYWALL

If you miscut a panel that has to fit around a utility box or into an inside corner and then force it into place instead of trimming it, the panel will likely blow out, tearing the face paper and cracking the gypsum within. This can also happen where a door or window frame has been misaligned with the partition line or at a corner that is significantly out of plumb.

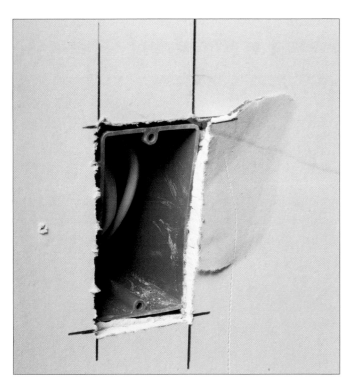

Fixing Broken or Blown-Out Drywall. *If a drywall panel hasn't been cut exactly to size around utility boxes and inside corners or if door and window frames are out of the partition line, the panel that is forced into place will likely blow out. This means that the utility box or an opposing piece of drywall will cause the drywall to break, causing the face paper to tear and the core of the drywall to crack. Fix blowouts by cutting away loose drywall with a utility knife and applying new layers of joint compound.*

To repair a blown-out section of drywall, cut away all the torn paper using a utility knife, and clean out the loose gypsum. Next, use a 5- or 6-inch knife to apply a coat of joint compound. Smooth this coat flush with the face of the panel; allow it to dry thoroughly; and then follow the usual three-layer taping procedure described in Chapter 6, page 97.

FIXING POPPED NAILS OR SCREWS

Nail pop refers to nails or screws that show their heads after the drywall job has been taped, finished, and painted. If nail pop occurs near the end of a drywalling job but before you paint, just the pressure of a paint roller can force a nail- or screw-head through the finished surface. Typically, however, nails won't pop until months after the drywallers, tapers, and painters have left.

Nail pop can occur wherever there is space between the back side of the panel and the face of the framing member to which it is attached. One of two events usually accounts for such a space: either the drywaller neglected to hold the panel firmly against the stud face while fastening it, or the stud contained excessive moisture when it was installed, and as it dried, it warped or shrank away from the drywall, leaving a gap. In either case, a slight pressure applied to the drywall face is all it takes. Sometimes, in fact, nail pop doesn't require even that: nail- or screw-heads can reveal themselves with the normal shrinkage of framing lumber as the house dries out over its first year, especially during the first winter, when it is heated.

If you have the opportunity, take preventive measures. First, if possible, frame with stable lumber that has been dried to the proper moisture content. When

The Pros Know

Like most other kinds of paper, the face paper of drywall panels will eventually yellow if left exposed to sunlight for too long. The yellowing may be slight, but it could still be enough, even after painting, for the contrast between white seams and yellowed paper to be seen. This is easily prevented: don't wait too long before painting. If the paper has yellowed, make sure to use a stain-killing primer paint.

hanging panels, apply mastic adhesive to the studs, and then drive in two nails at each location, spacing them about 2 inches apart. Make sure that you hold the drywall securely against the stud before driving nails or screws.

To fix a panel with popped nails or screws, first remove the protruding fasteners—or, easier still, drive them in farther until their heads sit just below the surface of the face paper. Next, drive screws or nails $1\frac{1}{2}$ inches above and below (or to each side of) the popped fastener. This will secure the drywall against the framing. Lastly, treat the area with three coats of joint compound, scraping each dry coat before applying the next. You'll notice that some nail pops will disappear on their own as the house expands and contracts from season to season. This often happens in new houses built with premanufactured roof trusses, which have bottom chords that expand and contract slightly as the house gains and loses moisture.

Drywall Repairs. One of the advantages of working with drywall is how easy it is to make minor repairs: most small dents and holes can be fixed seamlessly with just tape and joint compound.

Fixing Popped Nails or Screws. Nail popping can occur when framing members shrink behind drywall panels. If pressure is applied, as when walls are rolled with paint, the nails can pop through the joint compound or tape. Drive the protruding fasteners through, and then add additional fasteners $1\frac{1}{2}$ in. on each side to bring the drywall back against the framing.

Cleaning Up Dried Joint Compound

On a typical job, joint compound tends to end up all over the place. Gobs of this wet, sloppy substance fall to the floor or get splattered onto nearby walls. You'll find that "mud" cleans up much more easily when it's still wet. Simply scoop it up with a 5-inch drywall knife, and then follow with a damp rag or sponge to wipe up the remaining smear. If the joint compound has been left to dry, chip away at the hardened mound with the same tool. In most cases, it will break free. Again, follow with a wet cloth or sponge to get the last of it up.

Fixing & Repairing Drywall

FIXING CRACKS AND GASHES

You can repair stress cracks or minor gashes in drywall easily, using only joint compound and mesh tape. With most cracks, there is no need to cut out and patch sections of drywall; you don't have to provide backing if the cut does not go all the way through the panel. Simply treat it as though it were a drywall joint that you were finishing from scratch. Apply tape over the damaged area, and apply the customary three coats, sanding the final coat as necessary.

Tools and Materials

Difficulty Level:

- Utility knife
- Mesh or paper tape
- Joint compound
- 6- and 10-inch taping knives
- 120-grit sandpaper

1. PREPARE THE CRACK.

Clean out the crack by making a V-shaped cut along its length with a utility knife or small putty knife. Undercut slightly to create a *key* for the patching material to grab on to. Carve out all of the loose or broken gypsum, and clean off any torn face paper. Push on the panel around the crack. If the panel shows any movement, drive fasteners along each side of the crack into the nearest framing members. This will help to stabilize the panel and prevent further movement.

2. APPLY THE FIRST COAT OF JOINT COMPOUND.

If you're using mesh tape, apply it directly to the crack, and then spread a first coat (the rough coat) of joint compound over the tape. (If you're using paper tape, apply the rough coat first and embed the tape in it. Fiberglass mesh tape is recommended for fixing cracks, because the seams don't require strength as much as they do flexibility.) Smooth out the joint compound, feathering its edges. Let this coat dry completely.

3. APPLY SUBSEQUENT COATS, AND THEN SAND SMOOTH.

Using a taping knife as a scraper, knock down any burrs or high spots on the first coat. Then apply a second coat of joint compound, and let it dry thoroughly. Scrape down any burrs or high spots on this coat. Apply a third coat of joint compound; allow it to dry; and then sand this final coat with sandpaper or a sanding sponge to a finished smoothness.

2. *If you are using mesh tape, apply it directly over the crack before applying joint compound. Note that fasteners have been driven to either side of the crack.*

1. *Use a utility knife to clean out a crack before applying any joint compound.*

3. *As with seam finishing, the wider and thinner the final coat is layed on, the less obvious it will be on a painted wall.*

PATCHING A SMALL HOLE

Tools and Materials

Difficulty Level:

- Mesh or paper tape
- Utility knife
- 6-and 10-inch taping knives
- Joint compound
- 120-grit sandpaper

1. CLEAN THE HOLE, AND THEN APPLY THE ROUGH COAT AND TAPE.

Clean the drywall around the hole, cutting away all the loose or broken gypsum and trimming back any torn face paper. Apply two or three pieces of mesh drywall tape across the hole in an X pattern, or spread a coat of joint compound and embed paper tape.

2. APPLY A SECOND COAT.

Apply joint compound on top of the tape, smooth it out, and then carefully blend the edges into the wall. Let this coat dry completely.

3. APPLY TWO FINISH COATS.

Using a 6-inch taping knife as a scraper, knock down any burrs or high spots. Apply another coat of joint compound; smooth it out; and feather the edges down to the wall surface. After this coat has dried, knock down any burrs or high spots. Then apply a final coat of joint compound; allow it to dry; and sand it to a finished smoothness.

2. *Apply and smooth out the first coat of joint compound with a 6-in. taping knife.*

1. *For extra strength over a small hole, make an X with two pieces of fiberglass mesh or paper drywall tape.*

3. *Apply the finish coat of joint compound using a wider knife, and feather it out as thinly as possible.*

Fixing a Larger Hole. *The bigger the hole in the drywall, the more backing it will need to minimize stress on the finished joints and prevent the patch from falling back into the wall cavity.*

FIXING A LARGER HOLE

Tools and Materials

Difficulty Level: 🔨🔨

- Utility knife or saw
- Furring strips or wood blocks, drill, and screws
- Patching drywall
- Mesh or paper tape
- Joint compound and taping knives
- 120-grit sandpaper

1. PREPARE THE HOLE AND ADD BACKING.

Create a patch by cutting a squared-off section of drywall larger than the damaged area. Trace the outlines of the patch onto the wall. Use the outline to cut a square or rectangular opening in the wall. Cut furring strips or wood blocks that bridge the hole. You'll insert them behind the drywall panel to provide a screwing base for the patch.

2. FASTEN THE BACKING TO THE WALL.

Drive drywall screws through the panel around the perimeter of the hole to secure the furring strips or blocks. Use at least two screws per piece of wood.

1. *A rectangular hole with straight, evenly cut sides will be easier to patch than a ragged one.*

2. *Install 1x3s behind the hole so that they span its full width, with an overlap of 1½ in. to either side.*

3. ATTACH THE PATCH TO THE BACKING

Trim the patch to make it slightly smaller than the hole you've cut into the wall; you can fill any small gaps with joint compound. Screw through the drywall patch and into the blocks or furring to hold it securely in place. Depending on the size of the patch, add a screw every 5 or 6 inches or enough to make sure the patch is held securely in place.

4. APPLY JOINT COMPOUND AND TAPE.

Spread a coat of joint compound to fill the gap between the patch and the surrounding drywall. Embed tape in this wet first coat, and apply a layer of joint compound over the tape, just as you would if you were taping a seam between two drywall panels. Smooth out the coat, and let it dry thoroughly.

5. APPLY TWO FINISH COATS.

Apply a second layer of joint compound on top of the drywall tape. Smooth it out, and carefully blend the edges into the wall. Let this coat dry completely. Knock down any burrs or high spots with a taping knife. Apply a third coat; allow it to dry; and sand it to a finished smoothness. Remember to feather the compound well beyond the original damage to help the patch blend with the surrounding wall.

4. *Apply a coat of joint compound to fill the gaps between the patch and the drywall panel, and then embed the drywall tape.*

3. *Cut a drywall patch, and screw it in place by driving screws into the furring strips beneath.*

5. *Apply the second coat after the first has dried. A thin final coat will make the patch appear seamless after it's sanded.*

PATCHING OVER A REMOVED UTILITY BOX

When you permanently remove a utility or switch box, there remains a small rectangular hole in the drywall. A patch this small doesn't need backing, because the joint compound will hold it in place. To keep this small, unbacked patch from falling through the hole, bevel the edges of both hole and patch to form complementary angles.

Tools and Materials

Difficulty Level: 🔧🔧

- Measuring tape
- Utility knife or saw and surface-forming tool
- Patching drywall
- Joint compound and taping knives
- Drywall tape
- 120-grit sandpaper

1. PREPARE THE HOLE.

Bevel the edges of the drywall around the perimeter of the hole so that they flare outward from the hole about ½ inch—the perimeter of the hole on the wall surface will now be somewhat larger than the perimeter of the hole in the back. Make the bevel approximately 45 degrees, but don't bother checking the angle for accuracy.

The Pros Know

When working with wiring, you'll need to exercise some basic precautions. If you're removing a receptacle, first remove the fuse or flip the circuit breaker for the box before you touch it— *and* check the box again with a voltage tester before you go at it with a screwdriver. Never bury a broken or unused box beneath the wall—always remount the box in a new location before patching the hole. Don't touch wires behind the wall, even if it's just to move them out of the way, without first testing them with a voltage tester.

2. CUT A PATCH TO FIT.

Measure the beveled hole, and then cut a piece of drywall that will cover it to the outside edges. Then bevel the patch piece on all four sides, matching the bevel angle to that of the hole. A surface-forming tool or a sanding block will help to quickly smooth and true up the beveled edges. Test-fit the patch, and trim it as needed.

1. *For a small patch with no backing, like the one shown here, first bevel the perimeter of the hole.*

2. *Cut the patch, and bevel its edges so that it will fit neatly, like a plug, into the hole.*

7 Drywall Repairs

3. COVER THE EDGES OF THE PATCH WITH JOINT COMPOUND.

Before inserting the patch, *butter* it by applying a sufficient layer of joint compound to all four of its beveled edges.

4. INSTALL THE PATCH.

Firmly push the patch into place so that the joint compound oozes out of the seams. Using a 5- or 6-inch drywall knife, smooth the squeezed-out joint compound, and add more if necessary to make enough for a bedding coat. Embed drywall tape in this wet coat; cover it with more joint compound; and carefully feather this layer down to the face of the drywall. Let this coat dry completely before moving on to the next step.

5. FINISH THE SEAMS.

First, use a 6-inch taping knife to knock down any burrs or high spots that appear on the previous coat. Then apply a second layer of joint compound on top of the seams. Smooth it out, blending the edges into the wall. Let this coat dry thoroughly. Scrape down this second coat, and then apply a third coat of joint compound. After this final coat has dried, sand it to a finished smoothness.

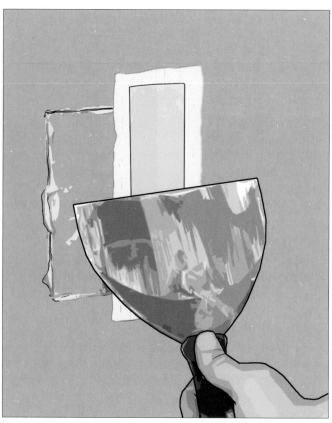

4. *After pushing the patch into the flared hole, coat and tape the entire patch and its seams.*

3. *Butter the edges of the patch with a substantial layer of joint compound.*

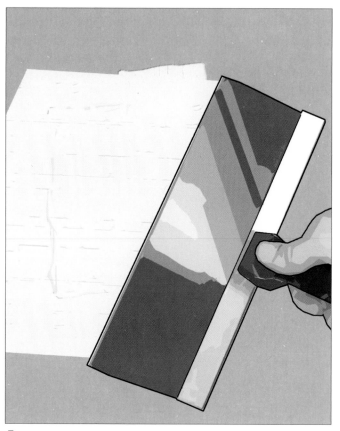

5. *The utility-box patch should be finished with a final, thin coat of joint compound, and sanded smooth.*

FIXING A HOLE USING WIRE MESH

To repair small holes without a wood-backed patch, you can use an old tradesman's trick. Thread one end of a 2-foot length of string through the center of a piece of sturdy wire mesh (known as hardware cloth). Tie that end of the string to a nail or small piece of wood to keep it from pulling through the mesh. Slip this mesh-and-string assembly into the hole, and pull the string taut so that the mesh presses against the inside of the surrounding drywall. While keeping tension on the string, apply joint compound. It will ooze through the mesh, holding it in place. After the first coat dries, cut off the string, and coat the patch as you would any small patch.

FIXING A UTILITY-BOX OVERCUT

Because utility boxes are small and so numerous in most drywalling jobs, it's quite likely that you will overcut the hole for at least a few of them, even if you use the coordinate method to position the hole. To fix an overcut hole, apply a layer of joint compound, squeezing it into the hole—some will stick to the utility box inside the wall and help support the patch. Cover this joint compound with paper or mesh tape, and then smooth more joint compound over the tape. After this layer has dried, follow it with two more coats of joint compound. Scrape any burrs or high spots between coats, and then finish-sand after the third coat has dried.

Fixing a Hole Using Wire Mesh. You can provide backing for a small patch by attaching a wood block to some wire mesh, inserting the mesh into the hole, and pulling on the string until the mesh is flush with the back of the drywall (top). Hold the string tight as you apply the joint compound (bottom).

Fixing a Utility-Box Overcut. Cutouts for utility boxes are easy to miscalculate but fortunately just as easy to fix. (Note the large gap at the bottom of the box in the top photo.) Butt the straight edge of a piece of paper drywall tape up to the edge of the utility box for a clean, straight patch (bottom).

PATCHING OVER A REMOVED WINDOW OR DOOR

Sometimes your project might call for taking out a window or door, or patching over a doorway to make a seamless wall. This calls for a large drywall patch. In projects like these, you'll need to frame the opening to provide sufficient backing for the patch and keep it from sagging between framing members, just as with ordinary drywall installation. For this application, space the framing 16 inches apart on-center, given that the patch needs as much support as possible. Make sure that the patch you install matches the thickness of the existing drywall. After fastening the patch, finish it using the customary tape (either paper or fiberglass mesh) and three-layer application of joint compound.

Tools and Materials

Difficulty Level:

- Standard carpenter's hand tools
- 2x4 or 2x6 lumber
- 10d nails
- Utility knife
- Drywall
- 1⅛-inch Type W drywall screws and screw gun
- Mesh or paper drywall tape
- Joint compound
- 6-inch taping knife
- 10- or 12-inch taping knife
- 120-grit sandpaper

1. PREPARE THE OPENING.

Remove the window or door and all the accompanying trimwork, and frame the opening with two-by lumber. If the existing wall contains insulation, install a comparable amount of insulation into the openings between the studs.

2. INSTALL THE NEW DRYWALL PIECE.

Measure, cut, and fasten in place a single piece of drywall that covers the opening.

3. APPLY A BEDDING COAT AND TAPE.

Apply a first coat of joint compound to the seams; then embed tape in the wet coat, and smooth it. Let this coat dry thoroughly.

4. FINISH THE JOINTS.

Scrape the first coat, and then apply a second coat of joint compound over the tape. Smooth it out, feathering the edges into the wall surface. Allow this coat to dry completely, and then knock down any burrs or high spots with a taping knife. Apply a third coat; let it dry; and then sand it to a finished smoothness.

1. *When a window (or door) is removed, frame up a structure that will serve to support a drywall patch.*

2. *Cut and install a drywall patch by nailing or screwing around its edges where it rests on the framing members.*

3. *Apply a layer of joint compound, and embed drywall tape into it while it is still wet.*

INSTALLING A LARGE PATCH WITHOUT FRAMING

Occasionally you'll encounter a large hole that won't need framing to support the patch. In this case, you'll still want to attach furring strips to the back side of the drywall to serve as backing. If the hole has an odd or ragged shape, start by trimming it to a square or rectangle. This will allow installation of a symmetrical piece of drywall. Make sure the patch's thickness is the same as that of the existing drywall.

Tools and Materials

Difficulty Level: 🦇🦇

- Framing square
- Utility knife
- 1x3 furring strips
- 1⅛-inch Type W drywall screws and screw gun
- Drywall
- Mesh or paper drywall tape
- Joint compound and taping knives
- 120-grit sandpaper

1. PREPARE THE HOLE.

Using a framing square as a guide, score around the rough hole with a utility knife to create a larger square or rectangular hole. Measure its dimensions.

4. *Finish the drywall joint as you would any drywall joint, with tape and a total of three coats of joint compound.*

1. *Ragged or asymmetrical holes need to be squared off. Cut a square or rectangle around the hole using a utility knife.*

7 Drywall Repairs

2. ATTACH FURRING TO THE WALL.

Cut 1×3 furring strips that are 3 or 4 inches longer than the vertical measurement of the opening. Insert them into the opening, and then screw (with Type W drywall screws) through the surrounding drywall and into the furring strips to hold them in place. Install a furring strip at each side of the rough opening and at least one in the middle. Space them no more than 16 inches on center.

3. INSTALL THE DRYWALL PIECE.

Measure the perimeter of the hole, and cut a drywall patch to these measurements. Then fit this patch into the opening. Screw it to the furring strips, using at least two screws (one near each end) and additional screws every 6 or 7 inches.

4. FINISH THE JOINTS.

Apply a first coat of joint compound to the seams, and embed tape in the wet coat. Smooth this coat with a drywall knife, and then let it dry thoroughly. After scraping, apply a second layer of joint compound over the tape. Smooth it out, blending the edges into the wall surface. Let this coat dry, and then scrape it to remove burrs and high spots. Apply a third coat; allow it to dry; and then sand it.

3. *Install a drywall patch, and screw through it into the furring strips beneath.*

2. *Install furring strips behind the wall, one on each end of the hole and one in the middle with a maximum on-center spacing of 16 in. Drive screws on each end of each furring strip.*

4. *Finish the seams of the patch as you would any other seams, with paper or fiberglass mesh drywall tape and three coats of joint compound.*

Providing Solid Nailing

Studs need to be padded with blocking *when a patch spans a full stud bay (left). These wood strips will act as a nailing or screwing base for a drywall patch and prevent it from sagging. If*

blocking is unavailable, cut down the midline of the studs with a utility knife to create a nailing surface for the patch (right). Be sure to locate and remove any fasteners before beginning the cut.

Fixing Cracks in Corners. *Structural movement in settling houses often first appears as cracks in inside corners.*

Some hairline cracks *can be simply covered or filled in with paintable silicone or latex caulk.*

FIXING CRACKS IN CORNERS

When drywall cracks in an inside corner, it usually means that the supporting framing has shifted or the foundation has settled. A new house often takes a year or more to settle out entirely, but older houses are still settling as well, causing cracks to appear—most often in corners. You can solve this problem one of two ways, depending on the size of the crack. If it's just a hairline, simply apply a bead of white latex silicon caulk. If the crack is larger, you'll need to apply joint compound with a large drywall knife (or inside corner knife) and smooth it to a sandable finish.

The Pros Know

If you decide to use caulk on the crack, just apply a bead and smooth it out with your finger. It is difficult to smooth caulk with a taping knife, so use this remedy only for small cracks that will allow you to wipe away the excess with your finger. Apply just enough caulk to fill the crack so that you don't have much excess to deal with.

Tools and Materials

Difficulty Level:

- Utility knife
- Joint compound (and paper tape if necessary)
- 5- or 6-inch taping knife
- 10- or 12-inch taping knife
- 120-grit sandpaper

1. PREPARE THE CRACK, AND APPLY A FIRST COAT.

Using a utility knife, clean out the crack, removing any loose joint compound. Then, with a 5- or 6-inch taping knife, apply a layer of joint compound, carefully working it into the crack. (In some cases, especially for large cracks, you may want to use tape as well.) Let this coat dry completely before moving on to the next step.

2. APPLY THE FINISH COATS.

After knocking down any burrs or high spots with a taping knife, apply a second layer of compound using a larger knife. Smooth it out, carefully feathering the edges to the drywall surface. Let this coat dry. Two coats may fill the crack adequately, but you might want to apply (and sand) a third coat if the patch still needs to be feathered into the face of the drywall.

1. *Cracks in corners may occur as framing shifts and dries, or when a structure settles. First clean out the area using a utility knife or small putty knife, and then apply a coat of joint compound with a 5- or 6-in. taping knife.*

2. *Use a wide taping knife to apply the second coat, feathering the compound into the wall surface. A third coat may be needed to complete the job.*

Drywall Resurfacing

Sometimes you may be faced with the problem of a wall that is too damaged to patch but not damaged enough to warrant demolishing the existing drywall and redoing the job. A situation like this may be caused by aging, water damage, or possibly numerous holes cut into a wall from an electrical or insulation job. Not only will making all these patches be time-consuming, but the odds are that the patchwork will still be visible once you've painted the walls. In this case, the best option to consider is drywall resurfacing: installing ³⁄₈-inch wallboard right over the top of the old with the help of adhesive and Type G drywall screws.

Resurfacing has other advantages over patching besides the time saved: it offers the finished appearance of a brand-new surface. Resurfacing also gives you the opportunity of opening up framing cavities to install new pipes, blown-in insulation, electrical circuits, speaker wire, or lines for an intercom system if you haven't already. Also, if the walls of an older home are covered with layers of lead-based paint, you can skip the costly removal, as the health hazard, which is only made worse by sanding or scraping the lead, will be concealed under the new surface. Repainting could contain any lead hazard temporarily, but the risk would resurface, literally, any time in the future when repairs or improvements involved sanding or scraping into the old layers of lead paint.

The main drawback to resurfacing walls is the extra thickness. Thicker walls can be a problem where the new material meets trim. The margin between the wall surface and the surface of the trim creates a raised edge. In an older home the edge thickness around windows and doors is likely to be ³/₄ inch or more, but newer homes may have less than ¹/₂ inch. This is why you should opt for thinner ³/₈- or even ¹/₄-inch-thick panels when resurfacing: ¹/₂-inch panels may end up being flush with your door and window trim, giving them an odd, recessed look.

While ¹/₄-inch panels might seem like the best choice, many remodelers don't use them because they are fragile and too easy to break—not once they are on the wall, but during construction when the panels are moved around, cut, and carried to the wall. Slightly thicker ³/₈-inch panels are often a better or at least more practical choice. Because these panels have more stiffness, there is less risk in handling, particularly when using oversize sheets—say, 10-foot or even longer lengths.

These final tips can help your resurfacing job go smoothly:

◣ Measure the total resurfacing area twice before ordering material. Plan ahead to accommodate delivery, immediate storage, and access into the room for oversize panels.

◣ If you are re-covering old drywall, don't install new drywall panels with seams directly over old joints.

◣ Save installation and finishing time by applying construction adhesive to the backs of panels and securing them with Type G screws instead of nails. Properly driven, these fasteners will leave a neat dimple in the drywall surface that is easy to finish.

7 Drywall Repairs

Drywall Resurfacing. *Heavily damaged walls can be given a brand-new skin with a thin layer of new drywall, applied with construction adhesive and Type G drywall screws (top). An easy way to install the new panels by yourself is by using starter nails—a few stuck into the panel can be tapped in with one hand while you hold the panel with the other (bottom). The rest of the fasteners can be either nails or screws.*

REPAIRING CORNER BEAD

Outside corners, especially those located in high-traffic areas between rooms, are prone to damage. The metal corner bead that's typically installed in corners (pages 89 and 112) helps resist some damage, but at times an accident can be severe enough to warrant the replacement of the corner bead.

In most cases, it is best to remove only the damaged section of bead rather than the whole corner. Use a utility knife to trace around the damage. This will prevent you from tearing the paper on the drywall panel when you pry off the damaged section of bead. Cut through the metal guard using a hacksaw or

aviation snips. You will need a pry bar or the claw end of a hammer to pry the bead away from the wall. Remove nails and screws as necessary.

Measure and cut a section of corner guard to replace the section you just removed. Install it using drywall screws or nails. Once the new section is in place, finish the corner with joint compound. Using the metal corner bead as a guide for your drywall knife, apply a thin coat to hide the bead. Apply a second coat when the first is dry. The trick with this repair is to feather the compound into the existing wall. Apply joint compound past the repaired section to help the patch blend in to the rest of the wall.

1. **Remove the Damaged Bead.** *After outlining the damaged area, use a hacksaw to cut out the damaged bead.*

2. **Cut a Corner Bead Patch.** *Using aviation snips, create a section of corner bead to replace the damaged one.*

3. **Install the Corner Bead.** *Use drywall screws or nails to hold the new corner guard in place.*

4. **Finish with Joint Compound.** *Let the raised edge of the corner bead act as a guide for your taping knife.*

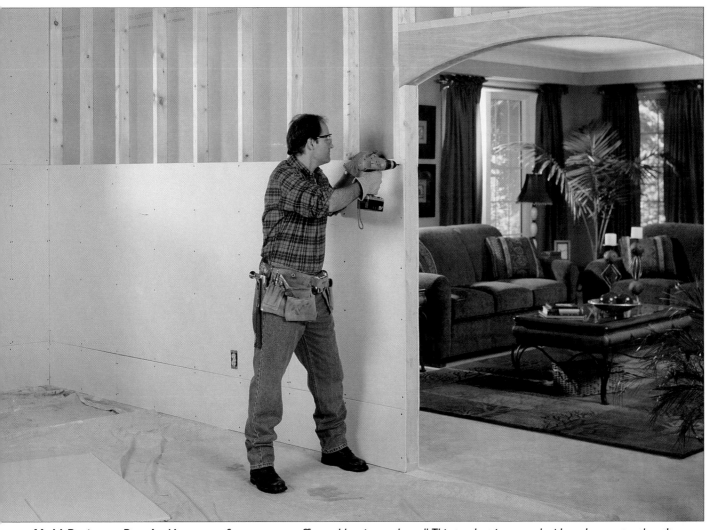

Mold-Resistant Panels. *Many manufacturers now offer mold-resistant drywall. This product is covered with a glass mat rather than paper to resist moisture and mold.*

Dealing with Mold

Mold can occur inside the home when mold spores land on a wet surface. The wet surface can be caused by a leaky roof, flooding, or high levels of humidity, such as those found in an unvented bathroom. In many cases, small amounts of mold are harmless, but some people are extremely sensitive to molds and can suffer severe allergic reactions, such as sneezing, runny nose, red eyes, and skin rash. If you are one of these people, leave mold removal to a pro.

Molds can grow on many building products, and drywall is no exception. In an extremely wet area, such as an area around a tub that is not sealed properly, mold can grow in wall cavities. There have even been cases where mold spores thrived under wallpaper. In some cases, the only way you know you have a mold problem is due to the moldy smell in the room.

The first step in solving a mold problem is to correct whatever is causing the wet area. If you get rid of the mold but don't correct the cause, the mold is sure to come back.

For small areas of mold, try cleaning with a household detergent. Wear gloves, and avoid breathing in the mold spores by working while wearing a N-95 respirator. It is best to seal off the room containing the mold so that spores do not travel to other areas of the house during cleaning. Avoid running forced-air HVAC systems.

Severely moldy sections of drywall should be removed using one of the methods discussed earlier in this chapter. Place moldy drywall in heavy plastic bags, and dispose of the bags in accordance with your town's waste-management procedures. Leave large-scale mold problems to a pro.

Fire Ratings

Fire-resistance ratings are given in hours; each number represents an hour that this construction will contain a fire and give protection from it under laboratory conditions. Sound transmission class (STC) ratings are given by the ASTM for sound-attenuating performance with regard to speech (not as accurate for mechanical noise, music, or other low-frequency sounds). The figure given is the minimum STC rating.

FIRE RATING	STC	DESCRIPTION	WALL SECTION
1 hour	30	Veneer plaster (approx. $3/32$ in.) on gypsum lath subbase ($1/2$ in.) on both sides of a 2×4 stud wall 16 in. o.c.	
1 hour	35	One layer $5/8$-in. Type X drywall on both sides of a 2×4 stud wall 16 in. o.c.	
1 hour	35	One layer $5/8$-in. Type X drywall on both sides of a $1 5/8$-in. metal stud wall 24 in. o.c.	
1 hour	40	One layer $5/8$-in. Type X drywall on both sides of a $3 5/8$-in. metal stud wall 24 in. o.c.	
1 hour	45	One layer of $5/8$-in. Type X drywall attached over one layer of $1/2$-in. fiberboard on both sides of a 2×4 stud wall 16 in. o.c.	
1 hour	45	Two layers $5/8$-in. Type X drywall on one side, and one layer on the other side, of a $3 5/8$-in. metal stud wall 24 in. o.c., with $3 1/2$ in. of fiberglass insulation in cavity	

FIRE RATING	STC	DESCRIPTION	WALL SECTION
1 hour	50	One layer ⅝-in. Type X drywall on both sides of a 2×4 stud wall 16 in. o.c., one side installed on resilient metal hat channel, with 1½ in. of mineral fiber insulation in wall cavity	
2 hours	50	Two layers ⅝-in. Type X drywall on both sides of a 2×4 stud wall framed 16 in. o.c.	
2 hours	50	Two layers ⅝-in. Type X drywall on both sides of a stud wall with staggered 2×4s, 8 in. o.c., on 2×6 plates	
2 hours	55	Two layers ⅝-in. Type X drywall on both sides of a stud wall with a double row of 2×4s, 16 in. o.c., on separate plates 1 in. apart, with 3½ in. of fiberglass insulation in wall cavity, and GWB fire stop in space between plates	
2 hours	55	2 layers ⅝-in. Type X drywall on both sides of 3⅝-in. metal studs 24 in. o.c.; one side has ¼ or ⅜-in. prefinished panels or laminating compound; 3½ in. of fiberglass insulation in cavity	
3 hours	45	¾ × 24-in. prefinished Type X drywall installed between 2¼-in. metal I-studs; other side has base layer of ⅝-in. Type X drywall perpendicular to studs, a 2nd layer of ⅝-in. Type X parallel to studs, a 3rd layer of ⅝-in. Type X parallel to studs, and then hat channel 24 in. o.c. perpendicular to studs, with 4th layer of ⅝-in. Type X perpendicular to channels, with 1-in. fiberglass insulation behind channels	

Recommended Levels for Drywall Finish

Four industry associations—The Association of the Wall and Ceiling Industries International, The Gypsum Association, Ceiling and Interior Systems Construction Association, and Painting and Decorating Contractors of America—have established a guide to drywall finishing based on the final decoration of the wall or ceiling. Here are the minimum requirements for each type of decoration.

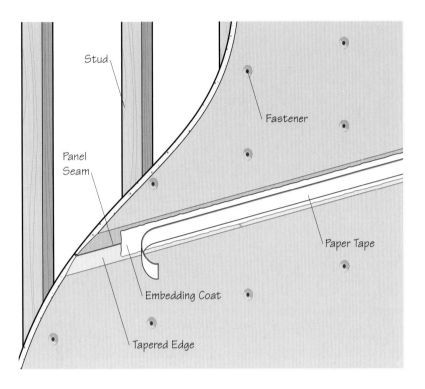

■ Level 1

All joints and interior angles shall have tape set in joint compound. Surface shall be free of excess joint compound. Tool marks and ridges are acceptable.

Frequently specified in plenum areas above ceilings, in attics, and in areas where the assembly would generally be concealed. Some degree of sound and smoke control is provided; in some geographic areas, this level is referred to as "firetaping." Where a fire-resistance rating is required for the gypsum board assembly, details of construction shall be in accordance with reports of fire tests of assemblies that have met the fire-rating requirement. Tape and fastener heads need not be covered with joint compound.

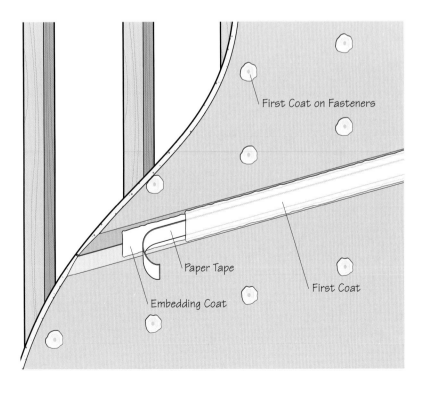

■ Level 2

All joints and interior angles shall have tape embedded in joint compound and wiped with a joint knife leaving a thin coating of joint compound over all joints and interior angles. Fastener heads and accessories shall be covered with one coat of joint compound. Surface shall be free of excess joint compound. Tool marks and ridges are acceptable. Joint compound applied over the body of the tape at the time of tape embedment shall be considered a separate coat of joint compound and shall satisfy the conditions of this level.

Specified where water-resistant gypsum backing board (ASTM C 630) is used as a substrate for tile; may be specified in garages or other similar areas where surface appearance is not of primary concern.

■ Level 3

Same requirements as Level 2 with one additional coat of joint compound applied over all joints, interior angles, and fastener heads. All joint compound shall be smooth and free of tool marks and ridges. Note: it is recommended that the prepared surface be coated with a drywall primer prior to the application of final finishes.

Typically specified in appearance areas which are to receive heavy- or medium-texture (spray or hand-applied) finishes before final painting, or where heavy grade wallcoverings are to be applied as the final decoration. This level of finish is not recommended where smooth painted surfaces or light to medium wallcoverings are specified.

■ Level 4

Same requirements as Level 3 with an additional coat of compound applied over all flat joints and fastener heads. An additional coat of compound over interior angles is not required. All joint compound shall be smooth and free of tool marks and ridges. Note: it is recommended that the prepared surface be coated with a drywall primer prior to the application of final finishes.

This level should be specified where flat paints, light textures, or wallcoverings are to be applied. In critical lighting areas, flat paints applied over light textures tend to reduce joint photographing. Gloss, semigloss, and enamel paints are not recommended over this level of finish. Unbacked vinyl wallcoverings are not recommended over this level of finish.

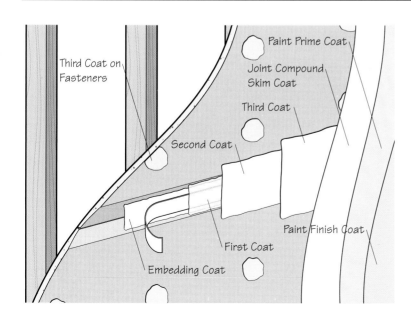

■ Level 5

All joints, interior angles, and fasteners, shall follow the requirements specified in Level 4. In addition, a thin skim coat of joint compound, or a material manufactured especially for this purpose, shall be applied to the entire surface. The surface shall be smooth and free of tool marks and ridges. Note: it is recommended that the prepared surface be coated with a drywall primer prior to the application of finish paint.

This level of finish is highly recommended where gloss, semigloss, enamel, or nontextured flat paints are specified or where severe lighting conditions occur. This highest quality finish is the most effective method to provide a uniform surface and minimize the possibility of joint photographing and of fasteners showing through the final decoration.

Resource Guide

The following list of manufacturers and associations is meant to be a general guide to additional industry and product-related sources. It is not intended as a listing of products and manufacturers represented by the photographs in this book.

Apla-Tech
W2024 Industrial Drive #3
Kaukauna WI 54130
800-827-3721
www.apla-tech.com
Manufactures pneumatic and continuous-flow drywall finishing tools. Visit the company's Web site for a full product line, as well as a detailed explanation of how its tools work.

Columbia Tools
1-5508 Production Blvd.
Surrey, B.C. V3S8P5
Canada
800-663-8121
www.columbiatools.com
Manufactures taping tools and accessories. Visit the Web site for a full line of taping tools and to read about product updates.

Dura-Stilts
800-225-2440
www.durastilt.com
Offers a variety of professional stilts. Visit the company's Web site to view products and product manuals.

EZRip
P.O. Box 1566
Vallejo, CA 94590
707-552-5510
www.buyezrip.com
Manufactures the EZRip drywall-cutting tool. The company's Web site offers testimonials, warranty information, and detailed information about the product.

FibaTape, a div. of Saint-Gobain Technical Fabrics
345 Third St., Ste. 615
Niagara Falls, NY 14303
www.fibatape.com
Manufactures sanding and drywall products. Visit the company's Web site for a full listing of product offerings.

Flannery, Inc.
300 Parkside Dr.
San Fernando, CA 91340
818-837-7585
www.flannerytrim.com
Manufactures specialty drywall and plaster trim. Visit the company's Web site for a full product catalog.

Georgia-Pacific
133 Peachtree St., NE
Atlanta, GA 30303
404-652-4000
www.gp.com
Manufactures building products and related chemicals. Visit the company's Web site to learn more about its drywall products, and to view its Education Station.

National Gypsum
2001 Rexford Rd.
Charlotte, NC 28211
704-365-7300
www.nationalgypsum.com
Manufactures and supplies building and construction products. The company's Web site features a complete listing of National Gypsum products, as well as resources for do-it-yourselfers and professionals.

Phillips Manufacturing Co.
4949 S. 30th St.
Omaha, NE 68107
800-822-5055
www.phillipsmfg.com
Designs and manufactures custom drywall, and metal and vinyl trim and beads. Visit the company's Web site for information on its products.

Pittcon Industries
6409 Rhode Island Ave.
Riverdale, MD 20737
www.pittconindustries.com
Manufactures decorative drywall panels. Visit the company's Web site for more information about its products, as well as an exhibition of its projects.

Trim-Tex
3700 W. Pratt Ave.
Lincolnwood, IL 60712
800-874-2333
www.trim-tex.com
Manufactures and distributes vinyl drywall beads and drywall finishing accessories. The company's Web site features a full catalog, as well as a gallery of projects using Trim-Tex products.

USG
www.usg.com
Manufactures and supplies building materials. The company's Web site features its history, product information, and a resource guide.

Vinyl Corp.
8000 NW 79th Place
Miami, FL 33166
800-648-4695
www.vinylcorp.com
Manufactures vinyl beads, trim, and control joints. Visit the company's Web site for a product catalog and information about price quotes.

West-Tech
#203 – 20628 Mufford Crescent
Langley, BC V2Y 1N8
Canada
604-534-0044
www.westtechtools.com
Manufactures taping tools and parts and accessories. You can purchase the company's products directly through its Web site.

Associations

Association of the Wall and Ceilings Industries (AWCI)
803 W. Broad St., Ste. 600
Falls Church, VA 22046
703-534-8300
www.awci.org
Provides services and offers information for individuals and businesses in the drywall and ceiling industries. The association's Web site offers a listing of events and programs, an online buyers' guide, and a page of helpful links for do-it-yourselfers and professionals.

The Ceilings & Interior Systems Construction Association (CISCA)
1500 Lincoln Hwy., Ste. 202
St. Charles, IL 60174
630-584-1919
www.cisca.org
Promotes the interests of the interior commercial trade industry. The association's Web site offers educational materials and resources.

Gypsum Association
810 First St. NE, Ste. 510
Washington, DC 20002
202-289-5440
www.gyspum.org
Promotes the gypsum industry in the United States and Canada. The Web site provides articles, publications, educational information, and industry statistics.

Glossary

Drywall construction and equipment—and the products associated with them—have been evolving for 60 years. Trade names are usually avoided in this book, and because tools and supplies often are linked to industrial names, we use generic terms currently in popular use. The definitions presented here apply to the context of this book only.

Abuse-resistant drywall A heavy-duty type of drywall—available in $\frac{1}{2}$- and $\frac{5}{8}$-inch thicknesses—that has heavier paper than regular panels and a reinforced core.

Arc Any portion of a circle, such as those found in an archway or curved wall.

Arch bead A plastic or metal strip designed to finish curved drywall seams in arched doorways or windows.

ASTM Formerly the American Society for Testing and Materials, now known by the initials; a nonprofit organization that publishes standards for various materials.

Backer board See *Cement board.*

Backing A stable surface to which a drywall panel can be nailed—either the framing members of the house, extra members that have been added, nailer blocks, or drywall clips.

Beveled edge See *Tapered edge.*

Beveled trowel Used for wide-coat applications, this tool resembles a mason's finishing trowel and has a slight bow so that it leaves a barely perceptible crown in the center of a coat of joint compound.

Blocking Lumber added between studs, joists, rafters, or other framing members to provide a nailing surface for sheathing or drywall.

Blown ceiling Popcorn-like texturing material fed through a hopper to an airless spray gun and blown onto a ceiling, where it is left to dry without retouching.

Blueboard See *Moisture-resistant drywall.*

Boom truck A truck with an articulated crane arm that can lift drywall to a second-story window.

Brocade A textured finish made by pressing a flat metal or wooden hand trowel into wet joint compound and quickly pulling it away.

Cement board Also called backer board and cementitious panel, this material is made with a portland cement core reinforced with polymer-coated glass fiber mesh embedded in both faces. Used as a substrate for tiles in wet areas.

Cement-coated nails Smooth-shanked nails coated with cement to increase resistance to withdrawal.

Chalk-line box A tool with a length of chalk-coated twine that is pulled taut across the face of a drywall panel or other surface and snapped to mark a straight line.

Circle cutter A tool used to make circular cutouts. The hand-operated type has a center pin through which slides an L-shaped arm with a cutting edge that you adjust to the desired radius.

Contact cement An adhesive used to attach vinyl-faced panels to a drywall base.

Cooler nails Smooth-shanked drywall nails.

Corner bead A length of thin-gauge galvanized-steel angle with holes drilled in its flanges, which is used to reinforce and protect an outside drywall corner.

Corner crimper A device used to set corner bead in place without nails. Hitting it with a mallet crimps the edges of the corner bead, setting metal burrs into the drywall panels that hold it in place.

Corner knife A two-faced knife that forms an inside corner and is used to finish corner seams.

Corner tape Flexible paper tape with 1-inch-wide galvanized-metal reinforcement used on outside and inside corners that form an angle greater than 90 degrees.

Deadman Also called a T-support or T-brace, this wooden device consists of a short cross brace at the end of a support that is slightly longer than the ceiling is high. It is used to pin and hold a drywall ceiling panel in place until it is fastened.

Drywall adhesive A product used to fasten drywall panels to wood or metal studs, or directly to concrete, masonry, or old drywall.

Drywall clips L-shaped metal braces measuring about 2 inches wide, which are used to attach partition walls to framing that provides insufficient backing.

Drywall hammer A hammer with a convex-faced head on one end and a tapered edge on the other. The rounded head creates a dimple in the drywall that can be neatly filled with joint compound. The tapered edge can be used to pry drywall panels in place.

Drywall jack Also called a panel lift, this caster-mounted tool is used to cradle a drywall panel, wheel it into position, crank it to the desired height, and hold it snugly in place for fastening.

Drywall nails Three types are available: ringed nails, cement-coated nails, and cooler nails, each of which has a minimum head diameter of $1/4$ inch.

Drywall saw A short, stout handsaw used to make long, straight cuts in drywall panels.

Drywall screws Three general types are available: Type W (for wood), Type G (for gypsum), and Type S (for steel).

Drywall tape Made from paper or fiberglass, it is applied to drywall seams or cracks as a base for joint compound.

Dust barrier A polyethylene sheet stapled or taped over an entry to prevent the escape of construction dust.

Dust-mist respirator A mask for the nose and mouth that filters out dust through a replaceable filter cartridge.

End-butt joint A seam where nontapered drywall panel ends or cut edges meet.

Factory edge See *Tapered edge.*

Fascia The vertical area between the wall-ceiling joint and the soffit.

Feathering The process of laying down a wide, thin layer of joint compound over a seam and sanding it gradually into the wallboard at the edges so that the mound of compound seems flat.

Fiberglass tape Also called mesh tape, this netlike material is adhered to a dry seam (with staples or its own adhesive) and then followed with a first coat of joint compound.

Filler coat The middle or second coat of joint compound in a three-coat application.

Finish coat The final coat of joint compound.

Fire-resistant drywall A type of drywall with a fiberglass-reinforced core that meets or exceeds the ASTM C36 rating for Type X fire-resistant gypsum board.

Fire wall A wall made with a type of $5/8$-inch-thick drywall that contains fire-retardant material.

Flexible bead L-shaped vinyl material used to finish a curved drywall edge, as in an archway or above a curved window.

Flexible drywall Drywall panels, $1/4$ inch thick, which are specially designed to withstand bending.

Foil-backed board Drywall laminated with aluminum foil (backed by kraft paper) to increase the drywall's insulation value and its effectiveness as a vapor barrier.

Framing members The structural elements of the house framework, consisting of studs, joists, plates, rafters, and so on.

Furring Softwood or stainless-steel strips, usually $2^{1/2}$ inches wide and $5/8$ or 1 inch thick (depending on desired stand-off), that are attached to studs or existing walls to create a flat backing for drywall panels.

Ghosting   See *Photographing.*

Greenboard   See *Moisture-resistant drywall.*

Gypsum   A mineral (calcium sulfate) that, after processing, forms the core of drywall panels.

Hawk   A wide, flat aluminum tray with a short handle used to hold joint compound.

Jab saw   See *Utility saw.*

J-bead   Edge-finishing material that wraps around the edge of a drywall panel to protect it from damage or disintegration; used where a drywall panel abuts a brick wall, a window jamb, or a shower stall. *Finishing-type* J-bead has a front flange that requires joint compound; *reveal-type* has a factory finish and is not meant to be used with joint compound.

Joint compound   A plaster-like substance used to fill seams and irregularities in drywalling, either the vinyl-based drying type, which hardens as the water medium dries, or setting type, which hardens by a chemical reaction that is catalyzed by water.

Joist   Framing lumber placed horizontally on edge, to which subfloors or ceilings are attached.

Laminating adhesive   A product designed to adhere layers of drywall in double-layer applications, and to attach drywall to concrete or rigid foam insulation (polystyrene or urethane).

Lath $1\frac{1}{2} \times \frac{3}{8}$-inch-thick softwood strips that are nailed to studs to serve as backing for plaster.

L-bead   Edge-finishing material used on a panel that abuts a door or window casing that isn't designed to cover a drywall edge.

Load-bearing   That part of a structure that supports the weight of the structure above it. Load-bearing walls are perpendicular to the rafters and joists.

Mixing paddle   A tool used to blend fresh joint compound.

Moisture-resistant drywall   Also called blueboard or greenboard; a moisture-resistant (not waterproof) type of wallboard that can withstand high levels of humidity, often used in bathrooms, kitchens, and laundry rooms.

MR board   Another term for *Moisture-resistant drywall.*

Mud   An informal term for joint compound.

Mudding   An informal name for the job of taping and finishing drywall.

Mud tray   A basin designed to hold joint compound during taping and finishing.

Nailer blocks   Wooden framing members inserted vertically or horizontally within stud or joint bays to provide backing for drywall panels that do not break on studs, joists, or furring.

Nail plates   See *Shields.*

Nail pop   The phenomenon of nails or screws showing their heads after the drywall job has been taped, finished, and painted, usually caused by shrinkage in the framing.

NIOSH   The National Institute for Occupational Safety and Health, a federal institute (part of the Centers for Disease Control and Prevention) that is responsible for conducting research and making recommendations for the prevention of work-related illness and injury.

Orange-peel finish   A textured finish created by applying watered-down joint compound with an airless sprayer.

OSHA   The Occupational Safety and Health Administration, a federal association (part of the Department of Labor) that is responsible for creating and enforcing workplace safety and health regulations.

Panel lifter   A device that resembles a miniature seesaw, used to lift a drywall panel 1 or 2 inches off the floor and hold it in position for fastening.

Partition wall   An interior wall that is not load-bearing.

Perforated paper tape Drywall tape with weep holes that allow joint compound to ooze through it.

Photographing When joint compound seams are visible through paint; curable by skim-coating.

Plasterboard A base material that provides a fire-resistant underlayment for trowel-applied plaster and has an absorbent face paper meant to draw water away from the freshly applied plaster to keep it from slumping.

Plate See *Sole plate; Top plate.*

Plumb bob A pointed metal weight with a string used to determine vertical alignment.

Pole sander A 4-foot pole with a swiveling plate to which sandpaper is attached, used to sand high walls or ceilings.

Powder-actuated fasteners Masonry fasteners that are driven using an explosive charge.

Radius The measurement from the center of a circle to the circumference; half the diameter.

Rafter The sloping beams used to support the roof.

Ridge The highest point of a roof.

Ringed nail A nail that is threaded to resist withdrawal.

Sanding sponge Fine-grained (120-grit or finer) polyurethane block sponge used to sand drywall.

Scriber A V-shaped, caliper-like tool with a pencil on one arm, used to transfer the contour of an irregular or out-of-plumb wall to a drywall panel, which is then cut to fit.

Self-tapping screws Type S drywall screws that have flanged tips, which enable them to drill quickly through 20-gauge steel framing. Screws without these tips can drill out larger holes in the drywall, making them more difficult to finish.

Setting-type joint compound Available only in powdered form, this type hardens faster than drying-type compounds.

Sheetrock U.S. Gypsum Co.'s trade name for gypsum wallboard.

Shields Also called nail plates, these 1×2-inch metal plates are applied to stud edges to protect wires or pipe running within studs from drywall nails or screws.

Shoe stilts Typically 2 feet tall, these devices strap to the shoes and lower legs and allow you to work from the floor rather than a ladder.

Skim-coating The technique of rolling water-thinned joint compound onto a wall and then flattening it with a 20-inch knife to create a very thin, paint-like layer.

Soffit The underside of a wall bump-out or an overhang.

Sole plate Also called the sill plate or mudsill; the framing member that rests on the foundation and forms the base of the walls.

Sound-attenuating See *Sound-deadening.*

Sound-deadening Any process that has the intention of reducing sound transmission between rooms, such as two-layer applications of specialty drywall and acoustical sealant, metal channels, and sound-baffling stud configurations.

Spackle A trademarked name for joint compound.

Staggered studs A framing method whereby studs are installed 8 inches on center on a 2×6 bottom plate, with alternating studs flush with each side of the plate.

STC (Sound Transmission Class) A numerical rating that quantifies the ability of construction systems to deaden sound; the higher the number, the more effective the system.

Straight-handled knife A 10- or 12-inch-wide rigid knife backed with a wooden or plastic handle and used to feather out wide joint-compound seams.

Stud Vertical two-by lumber that extends from the bottom plate to the top plate of a wall.

Stud finder An electronic device used to determine stud locations behind a wall.

Subfloor Plywood or other board that is installed on joists to form the base of the finish flooring.

Substrate Any material that supports another material that is bonded over it, such as backer board for bathroom tile.

Surface-forming tool A hand-held rasp-like tool used to shave $\frac{1}{8}$ inch or less from drywall edges.

Tape bender A tool designed to make a centered crease in drywall tape that is pulled through it.

Tape dispenser A drumlike tool clipped to the belt that dispenses drywall tape.

Tapered edge A slight, factory-milled bevel along both edges of a drywall panel's face side. When joined together, two such edges form a shallow, V-shaped recess that allows tape and joint compound to be finished flush with the panel face.

Taping compound A drying-type joint compound used for the first coat or, tape-embedding coat.

Taping knife A 5- or 6-inch scraper-like knife used to apply joint compound.

Textured roller A roller with a nap made from wire or plastic strands that leave a distinctive pattern in wet joint compound.

Toenailing Driving a nail at an angle into the face of a board so that it penetrates another board beneath or above it.

Tongue-and-groove panels Drywall panels with interlocking V-shaped edges.

Topping compound A drying-type joint compound used for the middle (filler) and/or finish coats.

Top plate The framing member(s) on top of a stud wall, upon which joists rest.

T-square A 4-foot aluminum square with a T-shaped fence. The fence has a lip on it that rests on the panel edge.

T-support See *Deadman.*

Type G screws Gypsum-type screws used to fasten drywall to drywall in a double-layer application.

Type S screws Steel-type screws used to fasten drywall to metal studs or furring.

Type W screws Wood-type screws used to fasten drywall to wood framing.

Type X gypsum board A drywall material that is fire-resistant.

Utility knife A razor knife with a retractable, disposable blade used for cutting drywall.

Utility saw Also called a drywall or jab saw, it has a round handle and serrated knifelike blade and is used to cut holes for utility boxes, pipes, and ductwork. The pointed tip is thrust through the drywall to start the cut.

Vinyl-faced panel Predecorated drywall paneling that is attached with adhesive and special fasteners and requires no edge or joint treatments.

Wallboard Another generic term for drywall.

Water-resistant drywall See *Moisture-resistant drywall.*

Photo Credits

Index

A

Abuse-resistant drywall, 15
Acoustical tiles, 49, 60
Adhesives, 22
Alignment, checking and
    correcting, 45, 46–48
All-purpose compound, 24
Arch, transfer, to drywall, 71–72
Arch bead, 20–21
Archways, 70, 97
    cutting out, 73
    installing, 96
Association of the Walls and Ceiling
    Industries International, 25
Aviation snips, 33, 56, 142

B

Backer board
    cement-based tile, 75
    cementitious, 103
    fasteners for, 103
    hanging, for tile, 103–104
Backing joints and edges, 44–45
Balloon framing, 10
Bathrooms, ventilation of, 18
Beam compass, 75
Bending radii, 97
Beveled edges, 19
Blown-out drywall, fixing, 127
Blueboard, 11
Boxed soffits, 62
Box extenders, fitting electrical boxes
    with, 54
Brocade finish, applying, 120–121
Broken drywall, fixing, 127
Brush and roller textures, applying,
    122–123
Building codes, 81
Bulging drywall, troubleshooting,
    126–127
Bullnose corner bead, 20

C

Calcium sulfate dihydrate, 10, 11
Calcium sulfate hemihydrate, 11
Cameo, 17
Cathedral ceilings, drywall for, 99–100
Caulk, use of, on cracks, 139
Caulking guns, 33
Ceiling Interior Systems Construction
    Association, 25
Ceilings
    checking and marking joists, 58
    drywall for cathedral, 99–100
    furring for, 51–58
    hanging sloped, 91, 92
    installing drywall on, 43, 83–84
    panels for, 17
    suspended, 26, 60
    hanging level channel for, 58
Cement-based tile backer board, 75
Cement board, 16
Cement-coated nails, 21, 82
Cementitious backer boards, 103
Cementitious panel, 16
Cement-panel joints, taping, 104
Chalk-line box, 30
Chalk lines
    marking straight cut lines with, 66–67
    snapping, 53, 55
Chisels, 31
Circle cutters, 33, 73, 74–76
Circular saws, 51
Claw hammer, 30
Combination squares, 31
Compass, 31
Contact cement, 22
Cooler nails, 21, 82
Coordinate method, 75, 76
Cordless drill, 32
Corner bead, 19
    metal, 89
    repairing, 142
Corner knives, 35
Corners. See also Inside corners;
    Outside corners
    creating floating, 92
Cracks

fixing, 128–130, 141
    preventing, at drywall joints, 99
    using caulk on, 139
Crowbar, 15
Curtain wall, 29
Curved cut lines, 70–74
    marking curves with template, 72–73
    marking round hole, 73–74
    marking semicircle with string, 71–72
Curved soffits, 60
Curved walls, hanging drywall on, 94–97
Curves, marking, with template, 72–73
Cutouts, making, with routers, 76

D

Deadman, 36, 78
    building, 37
Dens-Shield, 16
Dollies, homemade, 110
Dome suspension systems, 62
Doors, patching removed, 137–139
Double-layer systems, 13
Drywall, 9
    abuse-resistant, 15
    benefits of, 11
    for cathedral ceilings, 99–100
    defined, 10–11
    estimating, 24, 41
    fastening with nails/screws, 82
    fire-resistant, 14, 16
    flexible, 15
    framing dimensions and, 43, 44
    framing tips for, 43, 44–45
    hanging at inside corner, 87–88
    hanging on ceiling, 43, 83–84
    hanging on flat wall, 85–87
    hanging tips and techniques for, 78–81
    installing, 77–104
    on steel-framed wall, 93–94
    laying out job, 40–44
    length of, 13
    moisture-resistant, 15–16
    mold resistant, 143
    for odd-shaped areas, 100–101

ordering and storing, 11–13

plaster versus, 10

preparing steel framing for, 60–62

recycling, 75

resurfacing, 141

scribing, to irregular wall, 73, 74

selecting, 14

for stairway walls, 97–99

thickness of, 13

width of, 13

Drywall boxes, building around utilities or pipes, 102

Drywall clips, 20, 21, 88

Drywall hammer, 32

Drywalling screw guns, 32

Drywall jacks, 81, 99

raising panels using, 100

Drywall joints. See also End-butt joints

minimizing the number of, 40

preventing cracking at, 99

taping, on a flat wall, 107–109

Drywall knives, 121

cleaning, 116

Drywall layouts

10-foot wall, 41

16-foot wall, 41

20-foot wall, 42–43

Drywall repairs, 125–143

for bad end-butt joints, 127

for broken or blown-out drywall, 127

for bulging or recessed drywall, 126–127

for fixing cracks and gashes, 128–130

for fixing cracks in inside corners, 141

for fixing hole using wire mesh, 136

for fixing larger holes, 132–134

for fixing popped nails or screws, 127–128

for fixing utility-box overcut, 136–137

on installing large patch without framing, 140–141

for patching over removed utility box, 134–136

for patching over removed window or door, 137–139

for patching small holes, 131–132

for repairing corner bead, 142

Drywall ripper, 33

Drywall saw, 32

Drywall suspension systems, 26

Durock Cement Board, 11, 16

Dust control, 29

Dust masks, 28

E

Edge treatments, 19–21

Electrical boxes, fitting with box extenders, 54

End-butt joints

fixing bad, 127

flush, 40, 107

taping, 109

placement of, 43

staggering, 44, 45–46

Estimating, 24, 41

F

Face, 12

Fastener heads, finishing, 110–111

Fasteners. See also Nails; Screws

for backer board, 103

choosing the right, 54

masonry, 53, 54

powder-actuated, 53, 54, 55, 59–60

Fiberglass tape, 23

Finishing materials, 23–24

Finishing tools, 34–38

Finishing-type J-bead, 20

Finish-sanding, 114, 115

Fire-resistant drywall, 14, 16

Fire-resistant joint compound, 24

Flat walls

hanging drywall on, 85–87

taping joints on, 107–109

Flexible drywall, 15

Flexible metal corner tape, 21

Flexible vinyl corner bead, 20

Floating corners, creating, 92

Flush end-butt joints, 107

taping, 109

Foil-backed board, 17

Foot jig, 33

Framing

balloon, 10

for cement-based backer boards, 103

codes for, 44

drywall and dimensions of, 43, 44

furring over joist, 55–57

installing large patch without, 140–141

sound-deadening qualities of staggered-stud, 49

steel, 59–62

tips for, 43, 44–45

Framing squares, 31, 100, 101

Furring

attaching, to wall, 140

checking with string-and-block method, 53

installing metal, on ceiling, 57–58

over masonry or plaster, 52–53

over stud and joist framing, 55–57

pros on, 50

shimming, 55

of walls and ceilings, 51–58

Furring strips, 53

G

Gashes, fixing, 128–130

Ghosting, 123–124

Gypsum, 11

Gypsum Association, 25

Gypsum board, 9, 10

Gypsum lath, 17

Gypsum wallboard, sound-deadening qualities of, 49

H

Hammer-and-block method, 68–70, 76

Hammers, 31

Hand sanders, 35

Hanging and cutting tools, 32–33

Hanging materials, 21–22

Hardhat, 28, 29

Hardibacker, 16

Hawk, 35

Height, gaining, 36

Holes

cutting out, 74

cutting pipe, with pipe, 76

drawing, on the drywall, 73–74

fixing larger, 132–134

fixing with wire mesh, 135, 136

marking round, 73–74

measuring for round, 73

patching small, 131–132

Hole saw, 74–76

Horizontal blocking, need for, 45

Horizontal orientation, 43

Hydrous calcium sulfate, 10

I

Inside corners
    fixing cracks in, 141
    hanging drywall at an, 87–88
    taping, 112–114
    using J-bead on, 88–89
Installation, 77–104
    of archway, 96
    bending radii and, 97
    building drywall box around utilities
        or pipes, 102
    creating floating corner, 92
    creating sculptured effects, 90–92
    deadman in, 78
    drywall clips in, 88
    drywalling cathedral ceilings, 99–100
    drywalling odd-shared areas, 100–101
    drywalling stairway walls, 97–99
    drywall jack in, 81, 100
    drywall on steel-framed wall, 93–94
    fastening drywall with nails, 82
    fastening drywall with screws, 82
    hanging backer board for tile, 103–104
    hanging curved wall, 94–97
    hanging drywall at inside corner,
        87–88
    hanging drywall on ceiling, 83–84
    hanging drywall on flat wall, 85–87
    hanging outside corner, 89–90
    hanging sloped ceiling, 92
    hanging tips and techniques in, 78–81
    panel lifters in, 78
    scaffold in, 79, 80
    screws versus nails in, 81–82
    show stilts in, 81
    stepladder in, 79–80
    step-up bench in, 80
    using J-bead on inside corner, 88–89
    using J-bead on outside corner, 90
    using L-bead in, 89
    of vapor barrier, 104

J

Jab-and-dab techniques, 122
J-bead, 20, 88
    types of, 88
    using on inside corner, 88–89
    using on outside corner, 90
Joint compound, 23–24, 38
    blending, with masher, 106
    cleaning up dried, 128
    estimating, 24
    preparing, 24
    removing excess, 108, 109
    temperature of room and, 107
    weight of wet, 122
Joint tape, estimating, 24
Joist framing, furring over, 55–57

K

Kal-Kore, 17
Kerfs, cutting, 51
Kitchen, ventilation of, 18

L

Laminating adhesive, 22
Laser level, 58
L-bead, 20, 89
Level, 30
Level plane, checking for, 48
Lower-back support, 28, 29

M

Marking and cutting, 63–76
    curved cut lines, 70–74
        marking a round hole, 73–74
        marking curve using
            template, 72–73
        marking semicircle with string,
            71–72
        scribing drywall to irregular wall,
            73, 74
    cutting pipe hole with pipe, 76
    making cutout with router, 76
    recycling drywall, 75
    straight cut lines, 64–70
        hammer-and-block method in,
            68–70
        marking with chalk line, 66–67
        marking with T-square, 64–66
        using coordinate method for
    marking and cutting openings, 67–68
        using circle cutter, 74–76
        using hole saw, 74–76
Masonry, furring over, 52–53
Masonry fasteners, 53
    choosing the right, 54
Measuring and marking tools, 30–31
Measuring tape, 30
Mechanical finishing tools, 38

Mesh tape, fixing hole using, 129, 130
Metal and plastic accessories, 19–21
Metal corner bead, 89
Metal furring, installing, on ceiling,
    57–58
Metal snips, 56
Metal suspended ceiling systems, 60
Moisture-resistant drywall, 15–16, 18
Mold, dealing with, 143
Moldings, 17
Mold resistant drywall, 143
Mud tray, 35

N

Nailer blocks, installing, 44
Nail plates, 21
Nails, 21–22
    cement-coated, 82
    cooler, 82
    estimating, 24
    fastening drywall with, 82
    fixing popped, 127–128
    masonry, 53
    ringed, 82
    screws versus, 81–82
Niche, adding, 47

O

Odd-shaped areas, drywalling, 100–101
On-center stud spacing, checking, 47, 48,
    50
Openings, coordinate method for marking
    and cutting, 67–68
Orange-peel texture, 117–120
Outside corners
    hanging, 89–90
    taping, 113, 114–115
    using J-bead on, 90

P

Painting and Decorating Contractors of
    America, 25
Panel carrier, 28, 29
Panel jacks, 36, 80
Panel lifters, 33, 78, 91
    making, 33, 78
Paperless panels, 18
Paper tape, 23
Patches

installing large, without framing, 140–141

for removed utility box, 134–136

for removed windows or doors, 137–139

for small holes, 131–132

Pencils, 30

Perpendicular orientation, 43

Personal safety tools, 28–29

Photographing, 123–124

Pipe hole, cutting, with pipe, 76

Pipes

building drywall box around, 102

cutting pipe hole with, 76

Plaster, 10

versus drywall, 10

furring over, 52–53

Plasterboard, 9

Plaster of Pris, 11

Pliers, 30, 31

Pole sanders, 35

Polyurethane sponges, 35

Powder-actuated fasteners (PAFs), 53, 54, 55, 59–60

Power cutting tools, 33

Pros

on box extenders, 54

checking drywall joints for excessive crowns or recesses, 114

on creating circles, 73

on estimating number of panels needed, 41

on face paper of drywall panels, 127

on furring, 50

on hanging level channel for suspended ceiling, 58

on homemade dolly, 110

on installation, 85

on installing drywall on ceiling, 43

on joint compound, 122

on marking utility boxes, 69

on nails versus screws, 83

on preventing cracking at dry wall joints, 99

on steel framing, 57

on stock availability, 15

on taping inside corners, 112

on truss-built roof, 91

on using caulk on cracks, 139

on using T-square, 74

on working with wiring, 133

Q

QuickSet, 16

R

Recessed drywall, troubleshooting, 126–127

Reciprocating saw, 47

Recycling drywall, 75

Residential steel construction, 59

Resurfacing of drywall, 141

Reveal-type J-bead, 20

Ringed nails, 21, 82

Rocklath, 10, 17

Round hole, marking, 73–74

Routers, 74

making cutout with, 76

S

Safety

personal tools for, 28–29

with scaffolds, 79

Safety glasses, 28

Sanding pole, 35, 115

Scaffolds, 97

checklist for, 79

rolling, 79

using, 80

Screwdrivers, 30, 31

Screws, 22

estimating, 24

fastening drywall with, 82

fixing popped, 127–128

versus nails, 81–82

Sculptured effects, creating, 90–92

Semicircle, marking, with string, 71–72

Setting-type compound, 24

Sheetrock, 10

Shield-and-anchor systems, 55

Shimming, need for, behind furring strips, 51

Shimming furring, 53, 55

Shoe stilts, 36, 80, 81

Skim-coating, 123–124

Soffits

boxed, 62

curved, 60

Sound-deadening board, 17

Soundproofing, 49

Spanish-style finish, 121–122

Special finishes, 26, 116–123

brocade, 120–121

brush and roller textures, 122–123

job-and-dab techniques, 122

orange-peel texture, 117–120

skim-coating, 123–124

Spanish-style, 121–122

sprayed, 117

stucco, 121–122

Specialty bolts or pins, 53

Spirit level, 31

Sprayed finish, applying, 117

Square-edged drywall, 19

Staggered-stud framing, sound-deadening qualities of, 49

Stairway walls, drywall for, 97–99

Steel-framed walls, 59–60

installing drywall on, 93–94

Steel framing, 59–62

preparing, for drywall, 60–62

Stepladders, 79–80, 97

Step-up bench, 80

Straight cut lines, 64–70

marking with chalk lines, 66–67

marking with T-square, 64–66

measuring, 66

using coordinate method for marking and cutting openings, 67–68

using the hammer-and-block method, 68–70

Streel framing, 57

String, marking semicircle with, 71–72

String-and-block method to check furring, 53

String-and-block standoff method, 46

Stucco finish, 121–122

Stud adhesive, 22

Stud on-center spacing, 95

Studs

detecting misaligned, 48, 50

determining orientation of, 94

furring over, 55–57

padding, with blocking, 139

straightening, 50–51

Surface-forming rasp, 32

Suspended ceiling, hanging level channel for, 58

T

Tape, 23

Tape dispenser, 35, 36

Tapered edge, 19

Taping, 105–116

  applying joint compound, 12, 108, 109, 110–111, 113–114

  of cement-panel joints, 104

  checklist in taping prep, 106–107

  cleaning and maintaining, 116

  finishing fasten heads, 110–111

  finish sanding in, 114, 115

  of flush end-butt joints, 109

  of inside corner, 112–114

  of joints on a flat wall, 107–109

  of outside corner, 114–115

  removing excess joint compound, 108

Taping compound, 24

Taping knives, 34–35

Template, marking curves with, 72–73

Tiles

  acoustical, 49, 60

  hanging backer board for, 103–104

Toenailing, 50

Tongue-and-groove drywall, 19

Tool belt, 31

Topping compound, 24

Trowels, 34, 121

Truss-built roof, 91

T-square, 31, 100, 101

  marking straight cut lines with, 64–66

  using, 74, 75

Type G screws, 22, 81, 141

Type S scre-ws, 22, 81–82, 88, 93

Type W screws, 22, 81, 93

U

United States Gypsum Company (USG), 10

Utilities, building drywall box around, 102

Utility-box cutout locator, 69

Utility boxes

  coordinate method for marking and cutting openings for, 67–68

  hammer-and-block method for, 68–70

  marking, 69

  patching over removed, 134–136

Utility-box overcoat, fixing, 135,136–137

Utility knives, 32, 64, 65, 66, 67, 72, 74

Utility saw, 32, 33

V

Valleys, 61

Vapor barrier, 17, 103, 104

Vaults, 61

Ventilation, 18

Vinyl-faced panels, 17

W

Wall and ceiling prep, 39–62

  adding niche, 47

  backing joints and edges, 44–45

  checking and correcting alignment, 45, 46–48

  choosing the right masonry fastener, 54

  detecting misaligned stud, 48, 50

  framing dimensions and drywall, 43, 44

  framing tips for drywall, 43, 44–45

  furring walls and ceilings, 51–58

  getting the most from materials, 40–44

  installing nailer blocks, 44

  laying out drywall job, 40–44

  soundproofing, 49

  staggering end-butt joints, 45–46

  steel framing systems, 59–62

  straightening studs, 50–51

Wallboard, 9

Wall panels, finishing, 25–26

Walls

  checking for irregularities, 53

  checking for straightness, 57

  furring, 51–58

  hanging drywall for stairway, 59–60

  hanging drywall on curved, 94–97

  hanging drywall on flat, 85–87

  scribing drywall to irregular, 73, 74

  steel-framed, 59–60, 93–94

Wet-sanding, 115

Windows, patching removed, 137–139

Wire mesh, fixing hole using, 135, 136

Wire shields, 21

Wiring, working with, 133

WonderBoard, 16

Y

Yellowing of drywall panel face paper, 127

Metric Equivalents

Length

1 inch	25.4 mm
1 foot	0.3048 m
1 yard	0.9144 m
1 mile	1.61 km

Area

1 square inch	645 mm^2
1 square foot	0.0929 m^2
1 square yard	0.8361 m^2
1 acre	4046.86 m^2
1 square mile	2.59 km^2

Volume

1 cubic inch	16.3870 cm^3
1 cubic foot	0.03 m^3
1 cubic yard	0.77 m^3

Common Lumber Equivalents

Sizes: Metric cross sections are so close to their U.S. sizes, as noted below, that for most purposes they may be considered equivalents.

Dimensional lumber	1 × 2	19 × 38 mm
	1 × 4	19 × 89 mm
	2 × 2	38 × 38 mm
	2 × 4	38 × 89 mm
	2 × 6	38 × 140 mm
	2 × 8	38 × 184 mm
	2 × 10	38 × 235 mm
	2 × 12	38 × 286 mm
Sheet sizes	4 × 8 ft.	1200 × 2400 mm
	4 × 10 ft.	1200 × 3000 mm
Sheet thicknesses	¼ in.	6 mm
	⅜ in.	9 mm
	½ in.	12 mm
	¾ in.	19 mm
Stud/joist spacing	16 in. o.c.	400 mm o.c.
	24 in. o.c.	600 mm o.c.

Capacity

1 fluid ounce	29.57 mL
1 pint	473.18 mL
1 quart	1.14 L
1 gallon	3.79 L

Weight

1 ounce	28.35g
1 pound	0.45kg

Temperature

Fahrenheit = Celsius × 1.8 + 32

Celsius = Fahrenheit − 32 × ⅝

Nail Size & Length

Penny Size	Nail Length
2d	1"
3d	1¼"
4d	1½"
5d	1¾"
6d	2"
7d	2¼"
8d	2½"
9d	2¾"
10d	3"
12d	3¼"
16d	3½"

Have a home improvement, decorating, or gardening project? Look for these and other fine
Creative Homeowner books wherever books are sold.

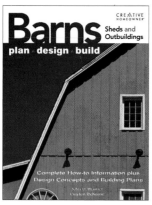

How to build and finish a utility building. Over 850 photos and illustrations. 240 pp.; 8¹/₂"×10⁷/₈"
BOOK #: 277812

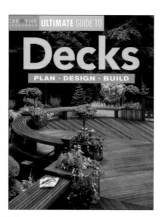

How to improve your home by adding a deck. Over 750 photos and illos. 288 pp.; 8¹/₂"×10⁷/₈"
BOOK #: 277168

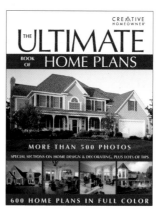

600 best-selling designs from leading architects. Over 500 color photos. 528 pp.; 8¹/₂"×11"
BOOK #: 277039

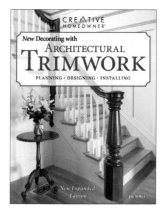

Transform a room with trimwork. Over 550 photos and illustrations. 240 pp.; 8¹/₂"×10⁷/₈"
BOOK #: 277500

How to work with concrete, brick, and stone. Over 800 photos and illustrations. 272 pp.; 8¹/₂"×10⁷/₈"
BOOK #: 277110

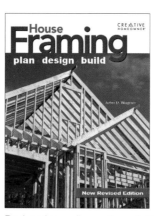

Designed to walk you through the framing basics. Over 650 illustrations. 240 pp.; 8¹/₂"×10⁷/₈"
BOOK #: 277660

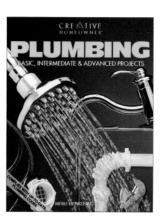

Take the guesswork out of plumbing repair. More than 750 photos and illustrations. 272 pp.; 8¹/₂"×10⁷/₈"
BOOK #: 278210

Best-selling house-wiring manual. Over 925 color photos and illustrations. 288 pp.; 8¹/₂"×10⁷/₈"
BOOK #: 278237

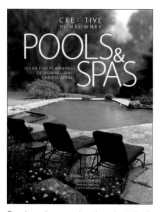

Pool and spa selection, installation, landscaping. Over 300 photos and illos. 224 pp.; 8¹/₂"×10⁷/₈"
BOOK #: 277853

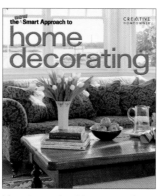

How to work with space, color, pattern, texture. Over 440 photos. 288 pp.; 9"×10"
BOOK #: 279672

Impressive guide to garden design and plant selection. More than 950 photos and illos. 384 pp.; 9"×10"
BOOK #: 274610

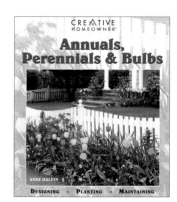

Lavishly illustrated with portraits of over 100 flowering plants; more than 500 photos. 208 pp.; 9"×10"
BOOK #: 274032

For more information and to place an order, go to **www.creativehomeowner.com**